The NORTH YORKSHIRE Cook Book

A celebration of the amazing food & drink on our doorstep.
Featuring over 40 stunning recipes.

The North Yorkshire Cook Book

©2016 Meze Publishing. All rights reserved.

First edition printed in 2016 in the UK.

ISBN: 978-1-910863-12-1

Thank you to: Andrew Pern – The Star Inn at Harome

Compiled by: Heather Hawkins

Written by: Karen Dent

Photography by:
Tim Green (www.timgreenphotographer.co.uk)

Edited by: Rachel Heward, Phil Turner

Designed by: Marc Barker, Paul Cocker, Matt Crowder

Cover art: Luke Prest, www.lukeprest.com

Contributors: Faye Bailey, Kerre Chen, Katie Fisher, Sarah Koriba, Bethan Littley, Holly Vincent
Printed by Bell and Bain Ltd, Glasgow

Published by Meze Publishing Limited
Unit 1B Kelham Square,
Kelham Riverside
Sheffield S3 8SD
Web: www.mezepublishing.co.uk
Tel: 0114 275 7709
Email: info@mezepublishing.co.uk

CONTENTS

FOREWORD

Yorkshire ... God's own pantry and the home of the awarding-winning Star Inn at Harome run by Yorkshireman Andrew Pern.

Having been born and bred in this fair county, I think I am fairly well qualified to fly the White Rose flag for the fantastic larder of food we have literally on our doorstep.

From the depths of the North Sea, our small coastal ports such as my hometown of Whitby provide us with an amazing selection of seafood and shellfish. I can still almost 'taste' the smell of Fortune's kippers wafting down the cobbled Henrietta Street under the shadows of Whitby Abbey from my memories as a very young child.

We lived on a farm just outside Whitby, where my father reared pheasants. I grew up watching the eggs hatch, later to become part of our 'rough shoot' and the cycle continued onto the Faisan à la Normande that I began to cook, with a can of cider and carton of cream from the village shop, at the age of nine.

Moving inland from the coast, we have the glorious purple-clad moors and their famous red grouse. Guns from around the world come for the much sought after feathered prize, and the partridges and pheasants from the local estates. They also feature on our menus during the season adding to the bag of brilliant produce.

The rich farmland of Yorkshire is perfect for rearing fabulous lamb, pork and beef outdoors, with many top quality rare breeds. The Vale of York brings us our asparagus, soft flavoursome strawberries and raspberries, amongst others.

When I think of the Dales, it's for the cracking cheese: Wensleydale, Swaledale, Yorkshire Blue, Harrogate Blue, Olde York. Yorkshire even produces the perfect snacks to combine with your cheese: Fat Rascals from Betty's or Yorkshire Brack from Botham's.

And to drink - a cup of Yorkshire Tea or, better still, a pint of Yorkshire ale. We have enough breweries in the county, large and small, to make you dizzy before you've tasted a drop!

Could there be a better location for our 14th century thatched pub? The amazing produce available in Yorkshire has helped it become one of just a handful of pubs in the world to be awarded a Michelin star, and is part of the reason that Yorkshire itself boasts the most Michelin-starred pubs and restaurants outside of the capital.

Obviously the warmth of Yorkshire hospitality has a major part to play and means that all the restaurants, pubs and other food-led eateries all have their own star quality too. So, start reading your way around the county - I know it'll be to your taste.

It ain't that grim up North tha' knows. It's reet grand. Cheers!

Andrew Pern

Pern ~ Chef Patron
Licensed Retailer of Wines, Spirits &
to be consumed on or off the Premises.
The Star Inn.

A Taste OF YORK

From regional treats to everyday essentials and superb meals in stunning venues, check out some of York's foodie attractions.

York and North Yorkshire are home to some of the foodie staples – and decadent treats – that are known and loved throughout the UK.

Originally a regional speciality, no self-respecting Sunday lunch is complete without a Yorkshire pudding. Equally, try imagining life without a decent cup of tea, some flavourful cheese, a bar of chocolate or a pint of beer, and you'll start to realise just how much the county and city have given to Britain's food and drink heritage.

Every chef and home cook has their own recipe for Yorkshire pudding. Originally served as a separate course, today's Yorkshires can be large puddings filled with the ingredients of a good roast, such as those served by the York Roast Co; added to a superb Sunday lunch like those made at York Tourism Awards 2016 best restaurant winner The Whippet Inn; or combined with pulled beef for a weekday lunch at the Walmgate Ale House.

North Yorkshire is well-known for cheese, from the traditional crumbly Wensleydale, to cheddar, gouda and bries produced with a Yorkshire twist. In York, Love Cheese has a café where visitors can sample these delights and more, and also makes superb bespoke wedding cheese cakes.

York is a chocoholic's dream. The city's chocolate heritage goes back to family firms such as Terry's and Rowntrees. You can discover more about the history at York's Chocolate Story, and find small artisan chocolatiers throughout the city.

To wash it down, you can't do better than a cup of Yorkshire Tea. First launched in the 1970s, it's made by family-run Taylors of Harrogate, whose business started in the 1880s.

If you prefer something stronger, North Yorkshire also has a fine brewing tradition. Within the city, the York Brewery creates handcrafted ales and is also a major tourist attraction.

York's abundance of exciting attractions mean it's firmly established on the tourist trail. And its foodie credentials guarantee gastronomic treats at many venues, whether you're after a luxurious afternoon tea inside the opulent restored Countess of York carriage at the National Railway Museum, or a hand-roasted coffee on the medieval city walls at Gatehouse Coffee. The Theatre Royal also has a fantastic new café and bistro, there's a beautiful Victorian atrium at the Bar Convent Café and No8 provides top class catering at the city's Art Gallery. Or settle down with a book, a cuppa and a slice of cake at the Rowntree Park Reading Café – Britain's first library-coffee shop.

The city's filled with venues to taste fantastic North Yorkshire produce. Shambles, once dedicated to butchers, is filled with eclectic foodie businesses; speciality food shop The Hairy Fig on Fossgate stocks local, continental and Mexican produce; and Ged Bell Butchers, further out of town sells locally-sourced meat and award-winning pies.

For something different, you can pick up the perfect spices for a home-cooked curry at Rafi's Spice Box; sample spirits, liqueurs, artisan oils and vinegars at Il Gusto, or choose a bottle to fill with your favourite drinks and oils at 'the liquid deli' Demijohn.

The city offers a taste of everything.

A Taste of York...
AND BEYOND

Explore local delicacies and exotic tastes on a global gastronomic tour of York.

York and the surrounding areas are chock-a-block with places where you can sit down to enjoy local produce at its finest. Whether your tastes are traditional or daring, a visit to the city isn't complete without trying some of the top-class eateries whose culinary net spreads across the globe.

The Star Inn the City is the little brother of the Michelin-starred Star Inn at Harome. It has a fantastic riverside location at the Old Engine House in the Museum Gardens, and mixes Yorkshire produce and hospitality from breakfast time through to evening meals.

Just outside of the city, a visit to Helmsley Walled Garden is essential if you're horticulturally-inclined. The garden grows fruit, vegetables and flowers and its edible produce can be sampled in the onsite Vine House Café. Originally built to feed the folk at Duncombe Park, the Walled Garden was a market garden until the 1980s, fell into a state of decay and was rejuvenated in the 1990s. It's a stunning experience for all the senses. Or visit Castle Howard's farm shop to discover local ingredients mainly sourced from within a 30-mile radius.

Organic vegetables from its own garden are also a major feature at Nunnington Hall. Lunches and afternoon teas are the order of the day at this stately home, which has its own tea garden for al fresco dining. The Balloon Tree, which has a farm shop and café, majors on home-grown produce too and serves superb award-winning cakes. The Holgate Windmill in York even produce and mill their own flour, which is used widely throughout local bakeries.

Top quality dining in and around York isn't restricted to British food. The city is truly cosmopolitan in its food offering and you'll discover a really international choice of eateries. You can go on a global taste adventure without leaving the city.

For a taste of India, head for the 29 States Indian Restaurant or pick up specially blended spice mixes to cook at home from Rafi's Spice Box. US cuisine is well represented by Byron Burgers, which serves simple, honest burgers made from British beef, while a trip to Las Iguanas takes you south of the border with flame-grilled Latin American dishes and sharing plates. Caribbean food and cocktails with a spicy kick are served up at Turtle Bay.

To try a taste of somewhere really off the beaten track, try Korean bistro and barbeque Oshibi or head to Yak & Yeti, a Gurkha restaurant majoring in Nepalese food. El Piano is a vegan venue with gluten-free options and a global menu using local ingredients.

York also has a vibrant European restaurant scene. Barbakan brings the traditional flavours and dishes of Eastern Europe to the city and Cotes Brasserie has French cuisine covered. Kapadokya is a family run Turkish restaurant, and Ambiente Tapas puts the spotlight on Spanish tapas, sherry and wine. Of course, every city needs a go-to Italian, and York has Delrio's Italian, where rustic tried and tested dishes are on the menu. For more information www.visityork.org/taste.

The Shambles

Castle Area

York's Sw...

Coach Rendezvous

Museum Gardens

Bedern Glaziers Studio

Treasurer's H...

Centenary Way

Afternoon TEA

Finding a venue that's just your cup of tea is no problem in York.

It's a trend that's swept the nation in recent years: refined afternoon tea with sandwiches, scones, cakes and a lovely cuppa – or even a glass of fizz.

But it's fair to say that York is probably the capital city of afternoon teas, and boasts a huge selection of venues serving this quintessentially British institution. Perhaps the queen of afternoon teas is Betty's. The tea rooms, which can now be found across the county, are a Yorkshire stalwart and in York, visitors can enjoy an extra special Lady Betty afternoon tea in the Belmont Room. Although afternoon tea is available all day every day at Betty's, the deluxe Lady Betty version – named after the tea room's cover girl who has been its mascot since the 1920s – is an exclusive pre-booked only affair that's the cream of the crop.

Afternoon tea in unusual surroundings is something that York prides itself upon. Transport yourself back in time to the era of elegant train journeys by taking your afternoon tea in the luxury of the Countess of York carriage at the National Railway Museum or take an afternoon tea cruise along the River Ouse with YorkBoat.

The Royal York Hotel, close to the station, is the perfect pit-stop for tea in the Garden Room before you head home. The Grange Hotel serves traditional afternoon teas plus champagne and sparkling wine varieties in the Regency-style Morning Room, and Middlethorpe Hall & Spa has an extensive menu of tea varieties to choose from to enjoy with your dainty nibbles.

For afternoon tea in café surroundings, try Crumbs Cupcakery close to York Minister where there's an amazing selection of luscious cupcakes to complement your cuppa. Cakes D'Licious in Clifton is a vintage-inspired tea room and cakery, where you can enjoy your tea inside or as a takeaway option.

Finally, if a themed event is more your cup of tea, the Grand Hotel & Spa doesn't disappoint: the Mad Hatter's Afternoon Tea takes you into Alice in Wonderland territory, from the table décor to the 'drink me potions'. The Dean Court Hotel, meanwhile, themes its cream teas around chocolate or Champagne. It's pure indulgence.

Cheese, Pies AND ALE

Traditional tastes of North Yorkshire from some of York's best producers and venues.

What could be finer than a handmade pie and a hunk of cheese, washed down with some proper Yorkshire beer?

If you're a real ale aficionado, you're in the right place. York boasts a thriving craft beer scene, with plenty of new producers using traditional techniques to create flavourful beers that can be enjoyed across the city and close by.

Perhaps the most famous is Black Sheep Brewery, run by the Theakston brewing dynasty. The brewer has its own visitor centre at Masham and its own spring under the brew house. York Brewery was set up in 1996 and makes authentic ales. It runs tours of the brewery so visitors can find out more about the brewing process. Ainsty Ales is one of the newest, founded in 2013 as a microbrewery with a vision to brew using as many local ingredients as possible.

You won't be short of places to sample real ales either. Sutlers opened in 2015 in an old Army & Navy store, while at the other end of the scale, The Guy Fawkes Inn is where the would-be destroyer of Parliament was born 1570.

The Three Tuns, which dates to the 1780s, is a Cask Marque pub, The Ackhorne has a traditional pub atmosphere with real ale on tap as does The Blue Bell Inn. While the very cool Evil Eye Lounge is known for its cocktails, you'll also find a great selection of beers. The Lamb and Lion's bar specialises in real ales and Walmgate Ale House serves up a super selection of steaks and beers.

You'll need something nice to nibble after sampling some of York's best brews, and you won't go wrong with a pie from Ged Bell Butchers. The butcher is known for its award-winning pork pies, which come with different toppings, and you can even pick up a pie with both cheese and ale encased in the pastry crust.

Cheese, of course, is a real food hero in North Yorkshire. Renowned for its regional Wensleydale cheese, the area also has a number of artisan cheese makers using traditional processes to create new and different cheeses. Love Cheese in York is the ideal place to sample a huge range of local cheeses, make up your own hamper or order a celebration cheese cake made to your own requirements.

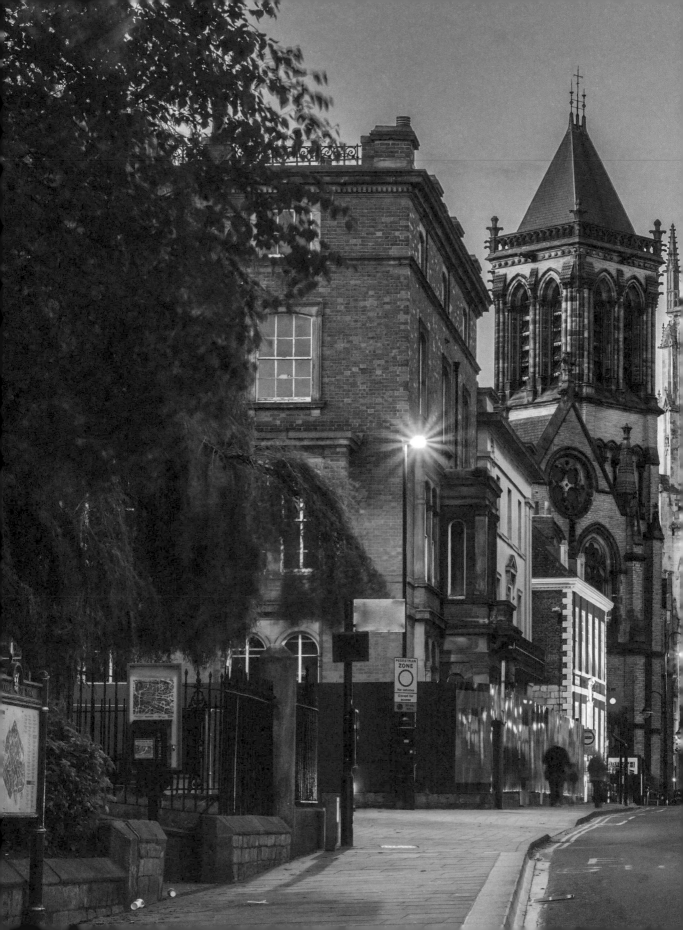

Chocolate CITY

York offers the ultimate experience for chocoholics to sample, make or just indulge in some of the finest chocolate you'll ever taste.

A trip to York isn't complete without delving into its chocolate heritage and sampling some of the decadent treats made in the city.

Quaker families, the Rowntrees, Terrys and Cravens built up a huge chocolate and confectionery industry in the city in the 19th century which still thrives today. Rowntrees – now part of Nestle – still makes Kit Kats in the city: an astronomical six million a day. Other iconic sweeties such as Yorkies, Aero and Smarties were invented here, along with Terry's Chocolate Orange, which actually started life as a chocolate apple.

The fascinating tale of chocolate from central America to York's role in its UK popularity is told at York's Chocolate Story, where there's also the opportunity to make your own chocolates and pick up treats made by master chocolatiers.

It's part of the city's special chocolate trail, taking visitors to sites around York associated with the sweet stuff and of course, calling in on newer artisan chocolatiers who are ensuring that the industry remains a big part of the city in the 21st century.

Monkbar Chocolatiers set up shop in 1999 and hand-makes its wares on the premises. You can select your own choice of chocs from a massive variety of flavours and fill a box to take home. York Cocoa House, which opened in 2011, is a chocolate emporium, which sells sweeties, runs activities and workshops and has a chocolate café. You'll also discover a branch of Hotel Chocolat in the city inside a beautiful Grade II listed building.

Chocolate plays a big part in York's food agenda. There are events and activities throughout the year, including a dedicated chocolate festival at Easter which kicked off in 2012 as part of the 150th anniversary celebrations for Rowntrees.

The whole York chocolate experience is so extensive that it can't be done justice in just one day. But one thing's guaranteed, however long you linger in the city, you'll be spoilt for chocolate choice, whether you're a fan of the much-loved Kit Kat, want to experiment with different flavours and textures, or fancy having a crack at making your own bespoke bar.

Festivals and MARKETS

Discover a wealth of new tastes at York's Food and Drink Festival and Shambles Market.

York's finest food and drink producers come together in one place every June and September for the city's annual food festival, which is one of the biggest in the UK.

Running since 1996, the food and drink festival takes over the city with its delicious sights, smells and tastes for a full week. Bustling markets, filled with locally produced cheeses, breads, cakes, chocolate and meats, take centre stage to the accompaniment of music and family entertainment.

Locally-brewed beers and Yorkshire-produced wines are available at pop up bars around the city, and you'll also find a scrumptious selection of street food. Regular venues get into the spirit of the event, with taste trails for food and ales, where you can explore some of the city's very best refreshments.

The cookery school is a central part of the festival, with lessons and demonstrations from chefs that'll inspire you to try some new ingredients and techniques at home. And of course, there are ample opportunities to taste new flavours and try new restaurants that offer special dinners and wine tasting events during the festival.

Throughout the year, the Shambles Market sells plenty of local produce, from meat and fish to artisan baked goods, confectionery, preserves, fruit and vegetables and street food. Foodie stalls rub shoulders with fashion, books, gifts and more in a vibrant, buzzing atmosphere.

Previously known as Newgate Market, a £1.5 million makeover introduced better lighting, weatherproofing and a new name in 2014. York has held markets since Viking times and the Shambles Market, which is open seven days a week, is one of the biggest in the North of England.

It's a must see if you're visiting York and it's also a popular shopping spot for locals. Regulars come for the chat and knowledge that stallholders who are there every day provide, while tourists have the opportunity to discover local ingredients – and local characters. A trip the Shambles Market provides a great opportunity to explore some of the tastes of York all in one place – and bag a bargain at the same time.

Cheese AND WINE

Pick up your favourite wine from Field and Fawcett Wine Merchants, then pop into the family's deli to pair it with the perfect artisan cheese.

Selling more than 800 different wines, 300-plus whiskies, 130-odd gins plus other spirits and local beers alongside a deli packed with Yorkshire and further flung ingredients, Peter and Cathryn Fawcett truly have a match made in heaven.

The Field and Fawcett Wine Merchant and Delicatessen is based in what was once the dairy at Cathryn's family-owned farm, just off the A64 at Grimston Bar near York. After more than two decades working in the wine industry, Peter decided to go it alone in 2006 and has made a name for himself as one of the North's top names in the industry.

He said: "I've been in the trade since the mid-80s, from a sales delivery driver and floor washer, to working in wineries in New Zealand in the early 1990s.

"My last job before setting up on our own was with a specialist business supplying into restaurants and bars. It was the last piece of jigsaw. I'd always wanted to do my own thing and Cathryn was very keen on the food side."

Peter, who has dual UK-New Zealand nationality, sells wines to bars and restaurants from Newcastle in the north to Chesterfield in south, as well as to individuals through the shop and nationwide via a thriving online business.

Local brews are in the mix too, with North Yorkshire beers and locally-distilled gins including Slingsby, Masons and Whittakers.

"The whole gin thing has gone crazy in the last few years," said Peter.

"There's an increasing cocktail culture among all generations now. Most towns will have a cocktail bar of some description but 15-20 years ago cocktails weren't part of the scene. Trendsetters are looking for something new and different and you can do a lot more with gin."

The local gins, alongside beers from Treboom, the Bad Seed Brewery, York Brewery and Raisthorpe Liqueurs are also available in the deli. Cathyrn stocks a great selection of Yorkshire produce such as Bracken Hill Preserves, Guppys Chocolate, Shepherds Purse, Ribblesdale Cheese Company cheeses and Reliance Salamis too.

She said: "Cheese is the big thing in the deli and you can pick a bottle of wine; the wine merchant and delicatessen goes really well together."

Field and Fawcett

Wine MATCHING

The team at Field & Fawcett Wine Merchants have recommended wines to match all the delicious dishes in this book.

AMELIA'S CHOCOLATES

Caramel Truffles

10-Year-Old Tawny, Niepoort (Douro, Portugal) £34.55

A good Port is a great way to end any meal. Many of us instinctively tend to pair it with a bit of Stilton but Tawny Port goes surprising well with chocolate. The prolonged ageing of this wine gives it a distinctive nutty, dried fruit character and Niepoort are truly the masters of this category. It's worth chilling ever so slightly to maximise the ripe red fruit aromas.

AMPLEFORTH ABBEY DRINKS

Ampleforth Abbey Beer Burger

The Den Pinotage, Painted Wolf Wines (Coastal Region, South Africa) £9.20

Pinotage is a tricky grape to get right. In the past it has suffered a deservedly bad reputation as a very low-quality varietal. When done badly it can be aggressively tannic and bitter but when grown in the right area the results are sublime. We think The Den is simply one of the best we've tasted. This wine was surely made with the barbecue in mind, it's a great partner to homemade burgers or sticky spare ribs.

AMPLEFORTH ABBEY DRINKS

Ampleforth Abbey Apple & Cider Cake

Darkwoods Under Milk Wood Coffee (Available in the Café)

Few things in our opinion share the same complexities that wine offers but we believe coffee could be one of them. Darkwoods source coffee beans from small, prime coffee-growing areas and look for farmers with the same passion for quality as some of the world's top wine-makers. Try the Under Milk Wood espresso blend which delivers wonderfully sweet caramel notes that are a perfect match to sweet baked apple flavours. What could be better than coffee and cake?

BALTERZEN'S AND NORSE

Cured Mackerel Tartare with Jersey Royals and Pickled Vegetables

Classic Manzanilla, Fernando De Castilla (Spain) £11.50

Mackerel is an oily, rich-tasting fish which needs rugged treatment in the kitchen and it needs a wine with similar power and snap. Sherry is not only great as an aperitif but also amazingly versatile with food. Powerful and acute on the nose, yet aromatic, intriguing and inviting. Sensuously textured rather than brittle, absolutely bone dry, aristocratic and very poised. This wine should tingle every taste bud in the same way as the dish.

BALTERZEN'S AND NORSE

Cinnamon Buns

Yorkshire Wolds Apple Juice £3.95

A wonderfully fresh apple juice from just outside the historic market town of Malton. Apple and cinnamon is a tried and tested classic and who am I to mess with a classic; serve and enjoy.

BARBAKAN CAFÉ AND RESTAURANT

Rabbit & Wild Mushroom Risotto with Parsnip Mousse

Langhe Nebbiolo, Produttori del Barbaresco (Piemonte, Italy) £16.95

Nebbiolo is one of those wines that demands to be paired with food, especially gamey dishes with mushrooms. This medium-bodied beauty from Produttori del Barbaresco combines bright red fruit aromas with hints of white pepper and aniseed.

BLACK SHEEP BREWERY

Steak and Black Sheep Ale Pie

East Bench Zinfandel, Ridge Vineyards (California, USA) £22.90

Ridge Vineyards is one of the world's most respected and recognised wineries. Their main focus is on Cabernet and Zinfandel planted high up in the Santa Cruz Mountains. The wine has a powerful nose of raspberry jam, pepper and violets. Firm acidity and a supple tannin structure work really well with richly flavoured, slow-cooked meats.

LE CAVEAU

Slow Cooked Yorkshire Rabbit in Cider

Côte de Nuits, Pascal Marchand (Burgundy, France) £21.50

Vibrant and complex as good Burgundy should be with fresh strawberry and rose petal perfume. The fresh acidity and delicate fruit character work brilliantly with classic bistro cuisine. An outstanding example of Pinot Noir from one of the great names of the region.

THE CLEVELAND CORNER

Baked Staithes Crab with Spicy Sweetcorn

Eden Valley Riesling, Pewsey Vale (Eden Valley, Australia) £13.40

Forget Blue Nunn and Black Tower, modern-day Rieslings are generally dry and full of character. The Eden Valley is one of the best areas in Australia for this style and Pewsey Vale regularly pick up the top critic awards. Dry, citrusy Riesling is brilliant with this dish. The aromatics work well with the spice and the limey zing complements the fish beautifully.

EAT ME CAFÉ

Caramel Pork

Passion Has Red Lips, Some Young Punks (South Eastern Australia) £11.90

Some Young Punks represent a new breed of winemaker in Australia, constantly seeking restraint and balance in their wines. This Cabernet/Shiraz blend has an electrifying nose of ripe red cherry and aromatic smoke. The uniqueness of these wines is very well represented by their increasingly outrageous labels.

EAT ME CAFÉ

Shetland Broch Pie

Veneto Rosso, Gran Passione (Veneto, Italy) £10.95

This dish cries out for rustic Italian red. Gran Passione is like a turbo-charged Valpolicella; at harvest, some of the grapes are left on the vines to dry in the sun. This adds more depth and spice to wine. Think prunes, redcurrants and roasted coffee beans.

THE FAIRFAX ARMS

Twice Cooked Belly Pork with Tomato, Chickpea & Chorizo Stew

Tres Picos, Bodegas Borsao (Campo de Borja) £13.60

As featured in the book "1000 Wines to Try Before You Die", this is one of the most highly rated Garnachas in the world. Generous yet balanced with black cherry and strawberry fruit, roasted herbs and peppery spice. A Spanish interpretation of Châteauneuf du Pape that goes perfectly with pork and chorizo dishes.

FILMORE & UNION

Chicken Tagine with Dates and Honey

Nagy – Somlói Furmint (Hungary) £9.95

Very rich on the palate, flavoursome, full of apricot and peach that will work wonderfully with the dates and honey without over powering. Floral with sweet spice and a touch of minerality on the finish. An unusual but great match.

THE GEORGE AT WATH

Panna Cotta, Honey, Granola and Strawberry Soup

Fragola (Wild Strawberry), Bepi Tosolini (Friuli, Italy) £23.50

Defined by a famous journalist from the specialised press as the "patriarch of the still", Bepi Tosolini is one of the world's great distillers. Its Fragola liqueur is packed with tiny wild strawberries and is a real treat with fruit desserts. Also, try adding a splash to a glass of Prosecco for some extra summer indulgence.

GISBOROUGH HALL HOTEL

Plate of Yorkshire Pork

Picnic Pinot Noir, Two Paddocks (Central Otago, New Zealand) £22.70

Pork and pancetta would normally cry out for a white wine, however the addition of black pudding and a red wine sauce changes the complexity and dominant flavours of the dish. A crunchy Pinot is the final piece to the flavour puzzle. Central Otago has been a home away from home for Pinot for a number of years now and whilst not always the cheapest by New World standards it is penny change by Burgundys. This vineyard is owned by actor Sam Neill whose parents were themselves winemakers. The wine's earthy, almost floral aromas will infuse beautifully with the fresh thyme and sage, and the wine's delicate fruit will ensure the pork and pancetta shine through.

THE GRANGE HOTEL

Yorkshire Curd Tart

Selection Chenin Blanc, Domaine Gayda (Languedoc, France) £22.50

When your food is rich, creamy and sweet with a wonderful zest then that is exactly what your wine should be. Domaine Gayda, under the watchful eye of Vincent Chansault, one of France's most exciting wine makers is producing scintillating wines throughout his range. The Selection Chenin is a medley of sweet fruit. Think apricot and mango with supple spice, the palate is richly textured but retains wonderful elegance and all important acidity which will complement the wonderful citrus of this dish beautifully. I promise you will not look at sweet wines in the same way again.

GRAYS COURT HOTEL

Fillet of Woolpots Farm Beef and Crispy Cheek, Little Oxtail Pie

Blau Marí, Moises Rovira (Catalonia, Spain) £9.50

A blend of ripe Garnacha aided by the structure of Cabernet Sauvignon that will really complement the powerful flavours of the dish. Flavours of sweet mulberry, with hints of dried fruits and tobacco. The name "Blau Marí" refers to the wine's Mediterranean origins and the ultramarine blue of the sea.

LOCKWOOD'S

Yorkshire Pork Cured in Smoked Paprika

Carmenère Reserva, Casa Silva (Colchagua Valley, Chile) £9.65

Over the last few years Casa Silva has been amongst the most highly awarded Chilean wineries. Its Carmenères are brilliantly bright and expressive with ripe blackcurrant fruit and hints of green capsicum and peppery spice. It typically has a certain smokiness which works brilliantly with barbecued or slightly charred meats.

NO8 BISTRO

Pheasant Kiev with Wild Garlic

Syrah, Elephant Hill (Hawkes Bay, New Zealand) £18.90

Hawkes Bay is perhaps better known for its Bordeaux blend reds but it seems to be their Syrahs that consistently catch our attention. This is quite a savoury style with lots of juicy blueberry fruit and aromatic, peppery spice. The savoury element of the wine works beautifully with gamey pheasant.

NO8 BISTRO

Thriller in Vanilla Sourdough

Chenin Blanc, Delheim (Stellenbosch, South Africa) £12.15

Chenin Blanc is really food-friendly. This is barrel-fermented which adds a bit of depth and texture on the palate. Notes of baked apple, quince and honey with some subtle vanilla oak undertones. If you were thinking of serving your sourdough with a rustic, gamey terrine then this is the perfect choice.

THE PHEASANT HOTEL

Poached Hotel Hens Eggs with Asparagus, Morels, Potata & Pea Shoots

Grüner Veltliner Haidviertel, Pfaffl (Weinviertel, Austria) £15.50

People should try to be less wary of Austrian wines; Grüner Veltliner is wonderfully aromatic and generally bone dry. This has lots of ripe mandarin fruit with a flinty mineral streak and just a pinch of black pepper. It pairs nicely with tricky ingredients such as eggs and asparagus.

THE PHEASANT HOTEL

Wild Halibut, Lincolnshire Prawn & Artichoke with Avocado & Sourdough Bread

Terlaner Classico, Cantina Terlano (Trentino Alto-Adige, Italy) £16.20

Alto-Adige is arguably one of the greatest wine regions on the planet, yet very few wine-drinkers are familiar with it. The area is best known for its white wines which show exceptional complexity and depth. Terlaner Classico is an unoaked blend of Pinot Blanc, Chardonnay and Sauvignon. On the nose green apple and white peach combine with fine nuances of lemon balm and mint. The texture of the wine works perfectly with the weight of this dish.

THE PHEASANT HOTEL

Strawberry Shortcake, Vanilla Cream Cheese, Strawberry and Rose Sorbet

Beerenauslese Sauvignon Blanc, Tschida (Neusiedlersee, Austria) 37.5cl £18.65

Hans Tschida was named "Sweet winemaker of the year" by the IWC (International Wine Challenge) four years in a row! He produces a full range of wines, right up to lusciously sweet delights like this heavily botrytised Sauvignon Blanc. A medley of heady aromas such as apricots, honeysuckle and lime marmalade characters; this is an excellent match for summer-fruit desserts.

THE PLOUGH

Salt Beef Salad Niçoise with Crispy Hen's Egg & Black Olive Flatbread

Collection Rosé, J. Mourat (Loire, France) £9.95

A blend of Pinot Noir, Cabernet Franc, Négrette and Gamay. This is like a more reasonably priced version of Provençal Rose, the wine the French would generally pair with this salad. The saltiness of the dish really brightens the red berry fruit character of the wine.

QUARMBY'S DELI
Emma's Carrot Cake
Whisky Pairing: All Malt, Nikka Whisky (Japan) £32.85

Japanese whisky is going from strength to strength at the moment and when the World's Best Whisky award was given to a Japanese distillery back in 2013, it's been harder and harder to get hold of. Fortunately, at F&F we have a great range to work through. The All Malt from Nikka is beautifully smooth, sweet and nutty with Christmas-cake spices, aromas of dark chocolate and just a hint of smoke. A rather decadent addition to a slice of cake in the afternoon.

QUAYSIDE FISH AND CHIPS
Fusco's Fish Pie
Muscadet Sevre et Maine Sur Lie, Vieille Vignes, Guy Charpentier (Loire, France) £9.50

Fish pie is the perfect excuse to bring out one of our old favourites. Some may view this wine-style as somewhat obsolete, but on the contrary, Muscadet is going through something of a renaissance at the moment with much more style and focus. Fresh, textured and delicately nutty it complements almost any fish cuisine.

RAFI'S SPICE BOX
Moghul-Style Roast Lamb (Shahi raan)
Koden Rioja, Bodegas Luis Alegre (Rioja, Spain) £8.95

Lamb loves Rioja! Especially one like this young crianza-style from the modern-thinking Bodegas Luis Alegre. A seductive nose of ripe black cherry and raspberry with undertones of toasty oak and vanilla.

ROBINSON'S CAFÉ
Chorizo, Parma Ham and Sundried Tomato Hash
Tannat, Pueblo del Sol (Canelones, Uruguay) £7.95

Tannat is traditionally grown in South West France and makes richly structured wines to pair with the local cassoulet. It is rarely seen anywhere else. It may come as a surprise then to see a Uruguayan Tannat. However, in recent times, the Uruguayans have been planting more and more of the variety and with great success. The wines are extremely soft and seductive and typically full of ripe plum and cassis aromas.

THE RYTHRE ARMS
Steak with Rythre Pepper Sauce
Recoleta Malbec, Mauricio Lorca (Mendoza, Argentina) £8.95

Some wine pairings are very simple and this is no exception. A good steak goes brilliantly with Argentinian Malbec. With peppercorn sauce it's best to look for something without too much oak like this fruit-forward style from Mauricio Lorca. This is everything you could ever want from a Malbec; dark, aromatic, fresh and super-soft.

SKOSH
Smoked Cod's Roe Cream, Salmon 'Caviar' and Potato Crisps
Gusbourne Brut Reserve Twenty Eleven (Kent, England) £32.90

Gusbourne Estate is continuing to blaze a trail in England's mission to make the world's best sparkling wine and winning countless awards on the way. The climate here as you would expect is very cool but this is perfect for sparkling wine production as it gives the wine wonderful acidity and pure fruit. Here we want the wine to add a splash of seasoning to the dish and the fruit and acidity will do just that, the wonderful texture and mousse of the wine will also ensure a wonderful harmony.

THE STAR INN AT HAROME
Grilled Black Pudding with Foie Gras, Apple, Scrumpy Reduction
Pinot Gris, Domaine Marcel Deiss (Alsace, France) £18.85

Domaine Marcel Deiss is one of the true wonders of the wine-world. Biodynamic vineyards are meticulously tended to by the expert hands of Jean-Michel Deiss. The exotic spice of his Pinot Gris works brilliantly with black pudding and the freshness of the wine is a great counterbalance to rich foie gras.

THE WHITBY DELI AND JUST JELLY
Lemon & Rosemary Chicken Risotto

"Gabriel" Pecorino, Terre di Chieti, Poggio Anima (Abruzzo, Italy) £8.95

Pecorino gets its name from Pecora which is the Italian word for sheep. Sheep in Abruzzo are particularly attracted to the variety as it's always the first to ripen. The wine has classic Mediterranean characters of wild herbs and ripe nectarines paired with a wonderfully waxy texture that works brilliantly with light risottos.

THE WHITE HART COUNTRY INN
Crispy Pork Belly, Black Pudding Croquettes with Apple Jelly and Smoked Cheese

FMC Chenin Blanc, Ken Forrester (South Africa) £23.85

I first tried this wine around a year ago and it blew me away. It is a bit of a house favourite at F&F and a trusty match with roasted pork. The wine is stunningly complex with notes of apricot, lemon curd, almond and even a touch of honey blossom. The palate is wonderfully rich, the fruit is pure with laser like precision. If you are looking for a show stopper look no further.

THE WHITE HART COUNTRY INN
A Taste of Yorkshire Rhubarb

Chateau Petit Vedrinnes Sauternes (Bordeaux, France) £10.95

Hand harvested over several passages through the vineyard to ensure only the best grapes reach the winery help create a wine that is not only wonderfully rich, but also wonderfully refreshing on the palate. When matching a wine to a dessert, rule one is to ensure the wine is sweeter. Swathes of baked apple, orange marmalade and honeysuckle, this will be an explosion of flavour.

YORK'S CHOCOLATE STORY
Raspberry & Orange Dark Chocolate Bar

Moscato d'Asti, Paolo Saracco (Piemonte, Italy) £13.60

Moscato d'Asti deserves to be recognised as one of the world's greatest wines, if simply for its capability to deliver pure sensorial pleasure. This remarkable wine displays a nose of white peaches and fresh grapes and a creamy sweetness that works even with the richest of desserts. Forget Asti Spumante - this is the real deal.

My Food
MEMORIES

Heather Hawkins talks about her earliest food memories
and being a Yorkshire lass.

My first vivid food memory was baking butterfly buns with my mum when I was about seven years old. I'm not sure how much of the baking process I got involved in. My role mainly involved hovering around the kitchen, holding the mixer a little bit and then indulging in my favourite part - licking the bowl. No doubt I sat by the oven impatiently waiting for them to bake.

I've always had a sweet tooth. My favourite food memory from going to the seaside were the doughnuts! Fresh and warm, sugary seaside goodness. Fish and chips always were a factor in our day trips but the doughnuts were what I remember so vividly and what nothing else can compare to. If I get a whiff of anything like it, I'm taken back in time to those hot summers. I have been known to drive to the seaside just for the doughnuts. Now that's dedication.

I've been fortunate enough to travel quite a bit in my pursuit of food. While in Paris I discovered macarons and ever since then, they've been my favourite indulgent and decadent dessert. On a trip to New York I sought out the independent foodies and definitely walked a fair few miles to indulge.

On a recent trip to Venice, I made a point of eating like the locals did to embrace the authentic way of life. This meant eating small dishes called cicchetti in the bacari (wine bars) for lunch. Then I indulged in true Italian pizza in my local trattoria, off the beaten track, and got to practise my Italian as well.

A lot of my social life revolves around food and drink in some way. Whether it's brunch at our favourite café, a cheese and wine night, or sampling my latest gin purchase, and I'm always the one who's asked to bring cake to a get together or make cupcakes for birthdays.

I also believe in supporting my local independent butcher, baker, cafés, and other food producers, it makes sense and I simply can't imagine not doing so. I always encourage my friends and family to do the same. After all, nothing else tastes quite like it.

I hope you love this book as much as I did compiling it. Being a Yorkshire girl myself, it has been a real pleasure to seek out the best of North Yorkshire.

Heather Hawkins

Amelia's Chocolate

Amelia's Chocolate
CARAMEL TRUFFLES

Make your own top-quality truffles as a gift, or just as an indulgent treat to enjoy yourself. Makes around 30.

From traditional favourites to best-selling chocolate letters and seaside-themed sweets such as chocolate fish and chips, Scarborough's Amelia's Chocolate offers a taste of something extra special.

Made from the finest Belgian Callebaut chocolate that's part of a fairtrade programme to ensure producers are properly paid and have access to healthcare, education and clean water, Amelia Scholey adds a local twist wherever possible. As well as the North Yorkshire flavour in the special Scarborough fish and chips, Amelia uses Wolds Way Lavender in her lavender drops.

Amelia, who underwent a heart transplant at the age of 15 due to a hereditary condition, began her career as an apprentice chocolate maker and rose to the ranks of master chocolatier. Her own business started life at her kitchen table in 2011 and she opened the shop in Victoria Road two years later.

As well as selling the luscious sweets, Amelia shares her skills with visitors: children's chocolate workshops during the school holidays, and night out parties and truffle workshops for adults. They certainly make a sweet evening out.

Ingredients

200g caramel flavoured chocolate drops

100g cream

500g milk chocolate drops

White chocolate or hundreds and thousands for decoration

Cocoa powder for rolling

Method

Melt the caramel chocolate drops and cream in a bowl in the microwave. Only microwave for 30 seconds at a time, making sure you give it a good stir every time.

Once it is all melted, smooth and shiny, allow to cool and then pop into the fridge to set. If you have the time, leave it overnight or put it in the freezer for about 20 minutes if you're in a hurry. When the mixture is set, roll it into around 30 small balls. Use cocoa powder on your hands to stop it from sticking.

Temper 400g of the milk chocolate by melting in the microwave to 45°c (use a digital thermometer to check), then using more chocolate chips bring it back down to 30.8°c. Only put a few chocolate chips in at a time and mix until they have all gone.

Once at 30.8°c, the chocolate is ready for you to dip your truffles in. Once dipped, place them on greaseproof paper to set.

You can decorate them with hundreds and thousands, scattering them on top as you go, or drizzle with tempered white chocolate once they are all dipped.

A sip of the
SPIRITUAL

Abbey beer, cider, spirits and juices are the fruits of centuries of expertise from Ampleforth's Benedictine monks.

More than 200 years ago, the Benedictine monks who arrived in North Yorkshire from France planted the orchard that today provides the apples used in Ampleforth Abbey Drinks.

Covering more than seven acres, and with 2,000 trees and 40 different types of heritage apples, it's the biggest commercial orchard in Northern England.

"The monks used the fruit for the monastery and school and as the orchards grew they began to have a surplus, so they started making cider," said Ampleforth Abbey Drinks' Emily Slingsby.

"The majority of the apples are dessert and cooking varieties rather than cider apples, and that gives a distinct flavour to the cider."

The cider is made on-site at Ampleforth's cider mill and has only been commercially available since the start of the decade. The orchard also produces brandies and an apple liqueur made from a blend of cider brandy and pure apple juice, which is also available to buy.

In 2012, Ampleforth revived the traditional monks' practice of brewing beer and is now home to the only traditonal abbey dubbel beer made in the UK. The seven percent strength drink uses an authentic Benedictine monks' recipe to produce a Belgian-style beer that's brewed on Ampleforth's behalf by Little Valley Brewery in Hebden Bridge. It's fast winning a loyal following from craft beer lovers.

Visitors to the Abbey, permanent home to over 40 monks, can find out more about the production of Ampleforth's drinks, book in for an orchard and cider mill tour and buy some bottles to take home. There is an on-site tea room, which uses the drinks in some of its recipes, and if the spirit moves you, you can join the monks in one of their six daily services, including Vespers where you can immerse yourself in their evocative Gregorian chanting.

Each October, the monks run an Ora et Labora – pray and work – retreat, where visitors spend the mornings learning how the monks live and pray, and the afternoons in the orchard bringing in the year's apple harvest.

So when you sip an Ampleforth Abbey Cider, you're enjoying the fruits of some very special labours.

Ampleforth Abbey Drinks

AMPLEFORTH ABBEY BEER BURGER

Proper hearty burgers packed with taste, texture and the unique flavour of
Ampleforth Abbey Beer. Serves 4.

Ingredients

For the burgers:

500g beef mince, 15% fat

75ml Ampleforth Abbey Beer

1 small onion

2 cloves garlic

1 slice white bread

1 egg, beaten

1 tbsp vegetable oil

Salt and pepper

To serve:

4 brioche buns

8 slices streaky bacon

Handful lettuce leaves

2 large tomatoes

200g cheddar cheese

Method

For the burgers

Place a medium sized frying pan on medium heat and add a drizzle of oil.

Dice the onion and crush the garlic and allow them to sweat in the pan. Cook until soft whilst ensuring they do not colour. Remove from the heat, drain and allow to cool.

Meanwhile, slice the crusts off the bread and discard. Grate the rest of the slice with a cheese grater to make breadcrumbs.

In a bowl, combine the mince, cooled onion mix, breadcrumbs, egg and the beer. Season with salt and pepper then mix everything together with your hands until well combined. If it is too wet, add some more breadcrumbs.

Take a little bit of the mixture and cook to check seasoning and adjust if necessary. Divide the mix into four and shape into burger patties.

Place a large frying pan on a medium-high heat, oil the burger patties and place in the pan with the bacon.

Cook the burgers for 5 minutes on each side. Once the bacon has cooked, remove it from the pan and leave to dry on a paper towel.

To serve

Slice the cheese and place on top of the burgers, add a splash of water to the pan and cover with a lid. Allow the steam to melt the cheese. Meanwhile, slice and lightly toast the brioche buns.

Place the burgers in the buns, adding the bacon and finishing off with sliced tomato and shredded lettuce along with your favourite condiments – we like to use Rosebud Preserves' Ampleforth Beer Fruit Chutney.

Serve your burgers with chunky chips and a side salad.

Ampleforth Abbey Drinks

AMPLEFORTH ABBEY APPLE AND CIDER CAKE

Fresh apple and cider combine to produce an intensely fruity taste in this easy to make cake, where you can amplify the apple flavour by serving with sweetened crème fraîche mixed with Ampleforth Apple Liqueur. Serves 12 with a 10 inch (25cm) round cake tin.

Ingredients

1 large cooking apple

330g self-raising flour

330g caster sugar

6 medium free-range eggs

275ml vegetable oil

65ml Ampleforth Abbey cider

To serve:

200g fresh cream or crème fraîche

10g caster sugar

A dash Ampleforth Apple liqueur

Method

Preheat the oven to 150°c.

Place the flour and sugar into an electric mixing bowl.

In a separate bowl, mix together the oil, cider and eggs. Pour the wet mixture into the dry ingredients and mix on a low speed for 5 minutes.

Peel the apple and cut into four pieces. Remove the core then cut each segment into three slices.

Grease the cake tin and line the bottom with parchment paper. Arrange the apple slices in the bottom of the tin and pour in the mixture.

Place the cake in the centre of the oven and cook for 1 hour.

Allow the cake to cool completely, remove from the tin, slice and serve with fresh cream.

Alternatively, for an even more intense apple flavour, serve with crème fraîche combined with a little sugar and a dash of Ampleforth Apple liqueur.

Scandinavian Inspired
YORKSHIRE SOURCED

Baltzersen's transforms from a Scandinavian café during the day into Norse,
a restaurant serving modern Nordic dishes in the evening.

Combining a mixture of Scandinavian-influenced food with great North Yorkshire produce and dishes adapted from a family recipe book that's almost 100 years old, Baltzersen's and Norse bring a unique flavour to Harrogate.

Named after owner Paul Rawlinson's Norwegian grandma, Liv Esther Baltzersen, the café serves until 5pm, then closes for an hour and reopens at 6pm as Norse. They are two distinct entities: Baltzersen's features café food with a Nordic flavour and Norse offers relaxed fine dining with four and eight course tasting menus.

Paul said: "Daytime is much more homely, laid back traditional fare I'd expect to eat if I was visiting relatives. Norse is a bit more involved and fancy – a modern interpretation of some Nordic influenced food."

The inspiration for the business were the meals Paul ate on holidays with his grandmother and he also uses updated versions of recipes that come from a book written by his great-grandmother in 1917.

"Most people would recognise most things because with Northern European cooking, there's a lot of crossover between dishes," he said.

"Some of the food I used to eat with my grandma when I visited but we always put a modern interpretation on it.

"Norse is a fine dining restaurant but much more casual and relaxed. Hopefully, we'll introduce people to something either new to eat or drink, different flavour combinations, products or methods of preparation."

The menu may have a Scandi slant but most of the ingredients are Yorkshire-sourced. That includes the Icelandic-style cultured yoghurt Skyr, which is made by Hesper Farm near Skipton from local milk.

The menu changes two or three times a week, and there's a great choice of cocktails, wines and craft beers to enjoy with your taste of Nordic cuisine.

Paul visited cafés in Norway before opening to get ideas for the inside of Baltzersen's. As a result, you'll find a mix of modern white tiling, rough cut wood, Scandi fabrics and artwork on the walls originating from both Yorkshire and Norway.

"We offer interesting and slightly different food, a nice place and lovely people who prepare and serve the dishes," said Paul.

FRESHLY BAKED CINNAMON BUNS

BALTZERSEN'S

Baltzersen's and Norse

CURED MACKEREL TARTARE WITH JERSEY ROYALS & PICKLED VEGETABLES

A taste of Northern Europe with tasty cured mackerel and pickled vegetables combining for a riot of flavours on your dinner plate. Serves 6.

Ingredients

For the mackerel:

6 mackerel fillets, skinned

80g sea salt

50g sugar

1 generous pinch chopped dill

1 lemon, zested

10g coriander seeds

Drizzle rapeseed or olive oil

For the dill skyr:

100g natural skyr (use natural yoghurt of you can't get skyr)

Pinch fresh dill, chopped, and ½ lemon, zested

For the crushed Jersey Royals:

1kg Jersey Royal potatoes (substitute a good quality new potato out of season)

200g banana shallot

1 clove garlic

1 tbsp lovage, chopped

1 lemon, zested

180g butter

For the pickled vegetables:

1 large red beetroot

2 large banana shallots

2 cloves garlic

100g each of caster sugar, white wine vinegar and water

5 Szechuan/white pepper corns 1 cinnamon stick, 1 star anise 1 tbsp coriander seeds, 1 bay leaf

Method

For the mackerel

Mix all the ingredients, apart from the mackerel and oil, together.

Cover the bottom of a tray with half the cure mix. Place the skinned mackerel evenly on top and cover with the remaining cure mix. Leave to cure for 30 minutes.

Rinse the cure mix off with water. Dry the mackerel by laying on a tea towel. Remove the bones down the middle with a knife ensuring you get them all.

Dice the boned mackerel into 1cm cubes and drizzle over the oil.

For the skyr (Icelandic yoghurt)

Mix the skyr, chopped dill and lemon zest together and place in the fridge.

For the crushed potatoes

Dice the shallots and garlic. Heat them gently in a pan with the butter until they start to soften, then remove from the heat and leave to cool for 10 minutes.

Simmer the potatoes in heavily salted water for approximately 15 minutes until tender. Strain and leave to cool slightly.

Add the shallots and garlic butter to the potatoes with the chopped lovage and lemon zest, then crush the mix with a fork. Don't forget to check and season accordingly.

For the pickled vegetables

Place all the ingredients apart from the beetroot and shallot in a pan with water and bring to the boil. Simmer for 20 minutes then leave to cool.

Cut the beetroot into 1mm thick slices then cut out with a 2cm metal ring cutter. Place the beetroot discs in a plastic tub and cover with half of the pickle liquor.

Peel the shallots, then slice into 2mm rounds. Separate the layers of shallot into rings and place in a tub with the remaining pickle liquor. Leave both the pickled veg in the liquor for at least 2 hours.

To serve

Place a 7cm metal ring in the centre of the plate, push one heaped tablespoon of the potato mixture into the ring. Put a teaspoonful of the skyr mix in the centre of the potato and a headed spoonful of the mackerel on top.

Arrange the pickled vegetables around the mackerel and dress with edible flowers, micro herbs or small watercress leaves to finish.

Baltzersen's and Norse
CINNAMON BUNS

Prepared the night before and baked in the morning, these cinnamon buns are
a real treat with a wonderful aroma that will fill the kitchen
while they're baking. Makes 12 buns.

Ingredients

For the dough:

900g bread flour

100g caster sugar

½ tsp salt

20g yeast

100g soft butter

410ml milk (room temperature)

2 eggs

For the cinnamon butter:

250g soft butter

250g brown sugar

25g cinnamon

To finish:

1 egg, beaten

Water icing made from 250g icing
sugar mixed with 2-4 tbsp water

Method

Add all the ingredients for the dough in a bowl and combine them, then knead for
10 minutes until the dough is stretchy and elastic.

On a floured surface, roll out the dough into a rectangle.

Combine the ingredients to make the cinnamon butter then smear it in a layer which is
just thick enough so that you cannot see the dough. Roll up tightly and double wrap in
cling film. Refrigerate overnight.

The next morning, preheat the oven to 160°c and unwrap the roll. Slice into 12 equal sized
buns and place on a greased baking tray.

Put the tray in a warm place to prove until the buns appear slightly wrinkled and bounce
back into shape when prodded.

Egg wash the buns and bake in the oven for 8 minutes. Remove from the oven, and using
a palette knife, press down firmly but carefully on any peaks that may have arisen during
baking.

Rotate the tray in the oven and bake for a further 6 minutes.

Once the buns are cool, put the water icing into a piping bag and follow the swirls on the
buns to finish.

A Taste of
EASTERN EUROPE

Traditional, hearty Polish meals, cakes and fresh-baked bread make up the diverse menu at Barbarkan Café and Restaurant.

Barbarkan Café and Restaurant brings the flavour of Eastern Europe to the centre of York, with a menu specialising in hearty Polish dishes.

Grzegorz Blasiak and Anna Witczak originally began the business as a small deli, but the popularity of their cakes, coffee and Polish favourites meant that Barbakan morphed into a café and restaurant in 2008. The venue is open for breakfasts through to evening meals.

Grzegorz is in charge of the baking and Anna cooks most of the meals. There is an astonishing range of 20-25 different cakes on offer, including traditional Polish poppy seed cake, Charlotte apple cake and a superb cappuccino cake that's similar to tiramisu. Grzegorz also bakes bread every day, and his sourdough loaves go down a treat with customers.

The delectable Polish pierogi dumplings, filled with beef or potatoes and cheese and topped with sour cream, is the bestseller on the café menu, and diners also love the traditional bigos – a hunter's stew stuffed with cabbage, wild mushrooms, meat and sausages. Borscht, served with wild mushroom pockets, is always available too alongside the soup of the day.

Grzegorz said: "It's hearty food and we have a lot of regular customers.

"Only 10-15 percent are Polish people – we have English, Chinese and Spanish customers too.

"People come in and ask about the dishes before they order, although some people are already familiar with the cuisine."

Although the provenance of the breakfasts, lunches and evening meals is Eastern European, Barbarkan sources its ingredients as close to York as possible. You'll also find Gressingham duck on the menu and the meat and vegetables come from local suppliers.

Inside, the ambience – like the food – is all about comfort, with wooden tables, glowing candles and colourful linens.

"It's a rustic, cosy place with lots of pictures on the walls," said Grzegorz.

Barbarkan Café and Restauran

COME DINE WITH ME

BARBAKAN
POLISH
RESTAURANT
01904 672474

Barbakan Café and Restaurant

RABBIT AND WILD MUSHROOM RISOTTO WITH PARSNIP MOUSSE

An Eastern European take on an Italian favourite,
with tender slow-cooked rabbit. Serves 2.

Ingredients

For the rabbit:

1 whole rabbit

1 medium carrot

1 leek

2 stalks celery

1 parsnip

Salt

Thyme, caraway seeds, marjoram and garlic to marinade

For the risotto:

Cooked rabbit meat

50g wild mushrooms – fresh or frozen fresh boletus edulis – porcini are best

60g hulled barley – from Eastern European or Polish shops, where it's called "pęczak"

500ml stock from cooking the rabbit

40g butter

1 medium banana shallot

100ml white wine

1 clove garlic

Fresh flat leaf parsley

2 tbsp of olive oil

For the parsnip mousse:

1 large parsnip

1 cup milk

1 tbsp mascarpone cheese

Fresh thyme

Salt and white pepper

Method

For the parsnip mousse

Peel and roughly dice the parsnip and place it in a small pan with milk and few stalks of fresh thyme. Cook for 10 minutes, discard the thyme and milk, and blend the parsnip with the mascarpone. Season with salt and pepper.

For the rabbit

Marinate the rabbit by rubbing in salt, garlic, caraway seeds, marjoram and thyme, then wrap it tightly in tin foil and place in a roasting dish.

Peel the carrot and parsnip and place in the tray with the leek and celery. Half fill the dish with water and cover with tin foil.

Cook in the oven at 180°c for two hours, then switch off the oven and leave the rabbit inside to cool completely. This makes the meat more tender and easier to remove from the bones. Watch out for small pieces of bone when removing the meat.

Discard the vegetables but keep the stock.

For the risotto

Heat a deep frying pan on medium heat with 2 tablespoons of olive oil and gently cook the diced shallot until translucent but not brown.

Immediately add the hulled barley and cook for another 3-4 minutes until lightly toasted.

Add the white wine and one clove of chopped garlic. Allow to reduce until the liquid is almost gone.

Add the mushrooms and rabbit meat (the whole rabbit will serve about 6 portions of risotto but it depends on you how meaty you want yours).

Pour the stock into the pan and reduce the heat. Cook for about 15-18 minutes, stirring occasionally until it's nice and creamy but still sufficiently liquid to flow freely – Italians call it all'onda, meaning 'wavy'.

Add the parsley and butter and stir until the butter has melted in.

Serve the risotto with a spoonful of parsnip mousse on the top. It goes well with fresh rocket and a drizzle of truffle olive oil.

Brewing
IN THE BLOOD

The sixth generation of the brewing Theakstons are sharing real Yorkshire ales with the UK from the Black Sheep Brewery in Masham.

Jo Theakston's family has been brewing at Masham since 1827, with the latest incarnation of the family business – Black Sheep Brewery – established by his father Paul in 1992.

The Theakstons' original family business was sold to Scottish & Newcastle Breweries in 1988, Jo and older brother and Black Sheep managing director Rob are sixth generation brewers.

Jo said: "Dad spent a couple of years kicking his heels but brewing was all he knew and that was in his blood, so he wanted to start again, ideally in Masham.

"Lucky there was a big old malting building available right in the middle of Masham, and he set about building a brewery from scratch.

"He didn't want a shiny, new brewery and had to find the kit to recreate a country brewery with traditional methods."

The equipment was transplanted from the defunct Hartleys Brewery in Cumbria and today, much of Black Sheep's beer is made with kit that's 75-years-old.

Black Sheep sells to customers across the UK and also exports. There's a huge range of traditional cask ales, bottled, craft, limited edition, small batch and seasonal beers, made with water filtered down from the Dales and collected from a borehole beneath the brewery, then combined with UK-grown hops and malt.

A recent introduction is a five barrel brewing plant to trial new beers without committing to the 50 barrel minimum made in the main brewery.

Jo said: "If we hit on a beer that works well, we can upscale into the bigger brew house, and if there's a demand, we can supply it in bigger volumes."

You can discover more about the brewing process at the Black Sheep visitor centre, which also has a bar, a shop and a bistro.

Jo, who joined the family business after working for other brewers, says there was never any doubt where his future would lie.

"My father was a master brewer and we'd go in at 7am while he mashed in the morning's brew, then jump in the car and go off to school," he said.

"When I was asked as a kid what I was going to be when I grew up, my thought was always 'what else would I do?' This is what we're born to do, and it was always in the blood."

Black Sheep Brewery
STEAK AND RIGGWELTER PIE

A family favourite flavoured with the unique Yorkshire taste
of Black Sheep Riggwelter Ale. Serves 4.

Ingredients

115g butter

Rapeseed oil

Seasoned flour

1kg braising, stewing, or chuck steak, diced

170g carrot, diced

170g swede, diced

170g celery, diced

½ onion, diced

1 bottle Black Sheep Riggwelter Ale

550ml beef stock

2 bay leaves

2 tsp thyme, fresh or dried

1 tbsp garlic purée (optional)

3 tbsp tomato paste

250g shortcrust pastry, or enough to cover your pie dish

Eggwash for the pastry

Method

Preheat the oven to 180°c.

In an ovenproof casserole dish, melt the butter with a drop of rapeseed oil on the hob. While it's melting, coat the meat in the seasoned flour.

Brown the meat in the butter/oil, then remove and set aside on a plate.

Add the diced carrot, swede, celery and onion to the casserole, sweat off, then remove and set aside.

Pour the Black Sheep Riggwelter Ale into the dish and reduce by half. When the ale has reduced, return the meat to the casserole and add the beef stock, bay leaves, thyme, garlic purée (optional) and tomato paste.

Add the vegetables you sweated off earlier, then put the lid on the casserole and cook in the oven for 1½-2 hours. The meat should be tender and still holding together, and the gravy reduced.

You can add 1 tbsp of corn flour mixed with a little water or beer at this point if you need to thicken the gravy further.

Transfer the mixture into a large pie dish or several small pie dishes and top with shortcrust pastry. Eggwash the pastry tops and bake for a further 15-20 minutes until golden brown.

Riggwelter Ale

Riggwelter Ale takes its name from a local Yorkshire Dales farming term which has Norse roots; "rygg" meaning back, and "velte" meaning to overturn. A sheep is said to be rigged or 'riggwelted' when it has rolled onto its back and is unable to get back up without assistance.

What better name for a strong beer from the Black Sheep Brewery in Yorkshire? Riggwelter is also available in cask. Bottled Riggwelter is available in many of the major supermarkets.

Bed, Breakfast
AND BISTRO

Based in the picturesque coastal village of Staithes, Cleveland Corner's bistro has a daily-changing menu where local seafood receives top billing.

It's not unknown for Cleveland Corner's chef and owner Rob Sim to run out in the middle of the evening. But don't worry – it's not because of the clientele in the tiny 16-seat bistro, it's because he's been called into action as a coastguard at Staithes.

It's one of the many strings to Rob's bow. He started his career as an actor, and worked as a street entertainer, fire-eater, juggler and a photographer before settling into the role of proprietor of Cleveland Corner with his wife Sharon.

The two have been at the helm of the two-room bed and breakfast and bistro in the beautiful coastal village that serves as the location for CBeebies show Old Jack's Boat since 2013.

Rob's a self-taught chef, who makes the most of the abundant local produce.

He said: "All the stuff we get is as local as possible. We're fortunate because there's a butcher who is just 20 seconds away and we get all our meat from him. There's a fishmonger at the top of the hill and we get seafood from him apart from the lobsters that come direct from the fishermen."

Fruit, vegetables and eggs come from the local shop and the menu changes daily to reflect the availability of seasonal ingredients.

"It's more fun and it keeps me on my toes if I'm not cooking the same thing day in, day out," said Rob.

"Some days, I buy something and think 'what am I doing with this?'

"We've always got a crab dish on. Staithes is very much known for crab and lobster and they are always available."

Cleveland Corner, which is so called because Staithes is on the border with the neighbouring county, has served food for at least 50 years in different guises. Under the Sim's stewardship, the little bistro is decorated from chair height to ceiling with a large and eclectic mixture of art that the couple have collected over the years.

"It's small, cosy, inviting and warm," said Rob.

"We wanted that sort of feel, where the odds are that you'll end up nattering to people sitting next to you. It's a proper night out; it's an evening's entertainment. It's not just somewhere to come and eat."

Cleveland Corner

Cleveland Corner

BAKED STAITHES CRAB WITH SPICY SWEETCORN

Crab is always available in Staithes and is always on our menu.
This dish brings out the sweet, subtle flavour of the meat while adding
excitement with the fiery sweetcorn. Serves 4.

Ingredients

For the crab:

25g butter (for dairy-free, use dairy-free spread)

1 banana shallot, finely chopped

½ red pepper, finely chopped

1 tbsp fresh dill, chopped, or 1 tsp dried dill

1 tbsp fresh parsley, chopped, or 1 tsp dried parsley

2 tbsp Parmesan cheese (for dairy-free, use soya cream)

½ tsp paprika

1 tsp lemon juice

50g soft brown breadcrumbs (you can use gluten-free breadcrumbs)

400g cooked crab, or 1kg or 2 x 500g live crabs

For the spicy sweetcorn:

25g butter (or dairy-free spread)

700g frozen sweetcorn

1 onion, finely chopped

1 green pepper, finely chopped

1 red chilli, finely chopped

1 clove garlic, finely chopped

1 tsp salt

A good pinch of paprika, pepper, oregano and thyme

100ml cream (or soya cream)

Method

For the crab

If you're using live crab, turn it upside down, lift up the small pointed flap and you'll see a small hole. Insert a knife (or screwdriver) into the hole and press firmly until it reaches the other side of the shell. Turn it back over and let the liquid drain out.

Half fill a large saucepan with well-salted water, bring to the boil and drop the crab in. Bring back to the boil and cook for 15 minutes for 500g or 20 minutes for 1kg of crab. Remove from the water and leave to cool.

Remove the claws and legs. Crack them open, trying not to let the shell shatter and remove the meat using a teaspoon or pick.

Put the body on its back/top, put your thumbs against the hard shell close to the crab's tail and prise the body section out and away from the shell. Discard the small grey stomach sack from behind the mouth and the long white "dead man's fingers".

Remove as much meat as you can from what remains of the crab. It's easier to do than to describe and don't be shy of the brown meat – that's where all the flavour is.

Preheat the oven to 180°c.

Melt the butter and soften the shallot and red pepper for approximately 8 minutes.

Add the dill, parsley, Parmesan, paprika, lemon and breadcrumbs and mix well.

Pack into 4 oiled crab shells or ramekins and bake for 10 minutes.

For the sweetcorn

Melt the butter and add everything except the cream. Cook for 10 minutes, then add the cream and heat for 2 minutes.

Serve with the baked crab.

Global GOODIES

Scarborough's Eat Me is anything but a typical seaside café, combining worldwide flavours with an underlying Scottish theme and a kooky retro ambience.

A mixture of international tastes with a definite Scottish flavour woven through the menu, Eat Me Café is surprising on lots of different levels.

Even the name, which you'd immediately link with Alice in Wonderland, actually has a different provenance.

"We want you to eat us visually as well as food-wise," says Martyn Hyde, who co-owns Eat Me with Stephen Dinardo.

"We were driving around and we couldn't decide whether to call it the Hanover Road Café or Eat Me. We saw two elderly ladies, so we stopped the car and asked them. They liked Eat Me best."

Located just behind Scarborough's famous Stephen Joseph Theatre, Eat Me is a community café with a loyal local clientele rather than tourists visiting the seaside.

The diverse menu, which ranges from Japanese Ramen and Thai dishes to Shetland pies, earned it The Good Food Guide's Best Café in the UK in 2014 award. Eat Me also has its own blend of coffee created specially by the Heavenly Coffee Company and a massive array of cakes baked every day.

Martyn said: "I've drawn on my experience living all over world in New York, Hong Kong and Thailand. My food is a mixture of many things and the Scottish flair is there because of Stephen, who is from Shetland.

"We use the Shetland Pie Company name, which are our own homemade pies, and they all have Scottish and Shetland themed names. Our Broch pie is the one that people love – it's spiced mince with nutmeg and a green onion and cheese mash on top.

"It's not the usual fare you get in a café in a seaside town."

Renowned for its generous portions, the majority of the food is made on the premises using local and seasonal produce whenever possible. Although the strong Asian influences means some of the ingredients can't be sourced in North Yorkshire, the pastes for the curries are all created in the Eat Me kitchen.

The café has what Martyn called a "kitsch-retro" vibe. Our tables are bespoke, styled to have the look of Asian food crates," he says.

"We like to serve things differently."

EAT ME

EAT ME CAFÉ

Eat Me Café
CARAMEL PORK

Sweet and sticky melt in the mouth pork with a taste of Asia. Serves 4.

Ingredients

75g Asian shallots, finely sliced

6 cloves garlic, finely chopped

500g belly pork, cooked, cooled and cut into thin cubes or slices

1 tbsp oyster sauce

1 tbsp light soy sauce

1 tbsp fish sauce

4 tbsp palm sugar

4 tbsp chicken stock or water

½ tsp ground white pepper

Vegetable oil, for deep-frying

Method

Heat 5cm of oil in a deep saucepan or wok over a medium heat and deep-fry the shallots until they are golden brown, taking care not to burn them.

Remove from the wok with a slotted spoon and drain well on paper towels.

Drain the oil from the wok, leaving around 2 tablespoons for shallow frying.

Stir-fry the garlic in the oil until light brown, then add the pork and stir-fry for a few minutes.

Add the oyster sauce, light soy sauce, fish sauce, chicken stock/water, sugar and ground pepper and continue cooking for about five minutes, or until all the liquid has evaporated and the mixture forms a thick, sticky sauce.

Spoon the pork and sauce onto a serving plate and top with the crispy shallots.

Caramel pork can be served with steamed rice and pak choi, or makes a fantastic filling for a Bao steamed bun.

Eat Me Café
SHETLAND BROCH PIE

A broch (pronunciation: ˈbrɒx) is an Iron Age drystone hollow-walled structure of a type found only in Scotland. Serves 4.

Ingredients

For the filling:

2 tbsp oil or lard

1 medium onion, cut into rough chunks

1 small swede, peeled and cut into rough chunks

1 clove garlic

450g lean minced beef

1 tbsp plain flour

1½ tbsp Henderson's Relish

1 tbsp tomato purée

1 tsp mixed spice powder

½ tsp dried thyme

300ml beef stock

Salt and freshly ground black pepper

For the smashed potato topping:

800g waxy potatoes, washed and cut into quarters

30g butter

50ml milk

2 spring onions sliced, green ends and all

Strong Cheddar, grated – as much as you like

Method

Put the onion, swede and garlic into a food processor and pulse until finely chopped.

Heat the oil or lard in a large saucepan, add the chopped vegetables and cook for about five minutes until soft and the onions are transparent.

Add the minced beef and using a wooden spoon, break up the mince but not to the point it becomes like sawdust; texture is all.

When the mince is thoroughly browned – and brown is flavour – add the flour and stir well.

Add the tomato purée, Henderson's Relish, mixed spice and dried thyme. Give it a good stir.

Add the stock and bring to the boil. Reduce the heat and cover, simmering for approximately 10-15 minutes.

The meat should be cooked and not too mushy. Add salt and pepper to taste.

While the meat is cooking, in a large saucepan, cover the quartered potatoes in salted cold water, bring to the boil and simmer until tender but not falling apart.

When the potatoes are cooked, drain well then smash with the butter and milk, but not too much as we like to leave a few lumps for texture. Stir the sliced spring onions through. Add salt to taste.

Preheat the oven to 200°c. Divide the mince into four large ramekins or one large pie tin, then top with the smashed potatoes. Leave the potatoes uneven and textured, this is going to add to the great crusty bits and be the roof of your broch.

Sprinkle the cheese over the top and bake for 20-25 minutes until your broch roof is crusty and golden.

Proper PUB FOOD

Steeped in history, The Fairfax Arms in Gilling East is a proper country pub with a proper Yorkshire menu.

When you visit The Fairfax Arms, you're keeping esteemed company. The pub, which is today owned by brothers Rob and Edward Fawcett, was built by English Civil War Parliamentarian general Sir Thomas Fairfax, who reputedly enjoyed a pint there with Oliver Cromwell before the Battle of Marston Moor in 1644.

"On the church opposite the pub, there's a corner stone where they allegedly sharpened their swords before they went," says Rob, who grew up in nearby Ampleforth.

"Peter Walker, whose Nicholas Rhea Constable books are the ones that Heartbeat is based on, is a visitor to the pub as well. He's a lovely chap; I've known him since I was a toddler."

The Fawcett brothers have been at the helm since the turn of the millennium and along with head chef Ben Turner, they have created a menu that has won awards for its Sunday lunches and is known for its variety. It's strong on pub favourites like steaks, bangers and mash and fish and chips, but there are also regularly changing innovative dishes and sharing platters.

Rob said: "I want to be able to read a menu and actually find I can't pick what I want, because there's that much I want. I want your mouth to be watering when you read the menu.

"We change it four or five times a year but we keep certain favourites because if we took them off the menu, we'd be lynched."

The pub sources meat from Easingwold butcher Geoff Thornton, who drinks at The Fairfax Arms, and its Himalayan rock salt aged steaks come from R&J Butchers in Ripon. There's a strong local flavour behind the bar too, which serves real ales from Black Sheep, Tetley's and guest ales from the nearby Helmsley Brewing Company. You'll also discover a great wine selection – "I take pride in the wine, I'm good at drinking wine," says Rob.

Attracting visitors to Ampleforth, who come for the glorious walking, and golfers using the nine-hole course in the grounds of Gilling Castle, The Fairfax Arms is above all a locals' pub.

"It's not our pub," says Rob. "It's the locals'; we're just the caretakers."

The Fairfax Arms

TWICE COOKED BELLY PORK WITH TOMATO, CHICKPEA & CHORIZO STEW

A superb slow-cooked supper dish that's worth the wait. Serves 4.

Ingredients

1kg belly pork

250ml Ampleforth Abbey Cider

250ml vegetable stock

200ml chicken stock

400g cooked chickpeas, drained

400g tomatoes, chopped

100ml Yorkshire rapeseed oil

2 onions, diced

2 cloves garlic, chopped

100g coriander, chopped

100g Yorkshire chorizo, chopped

1 tsp ground cumin

1 tsp smoked paprika

400g baby leaf spinach

Salt

Method

For the pork

The belly pork needs to be cooked 10 hours in advance. Preheat the oven to 150°c and rub table salt in to the belly pork skin, to give a better crackling.

Place the belly pork on a wire rack on a tray and pour in the cider and vegetable stock. Wrap the tray in tin foil and cook in the oven for six hours or until tender.

Once the belly pork is cooked, remove from the stock and place in between two baking trays. Press down with a heavy weight and place in the fridge for at least two hours.

When the pork has cooled, cut it into four pieces and reheat on a baking tray in the oven at 180°c for 20-25 minutes until the crackling is well ... cracking!

For the stew

Heat the oil in a heavy bottomed saucepan over a medium heat. Add the garlic and onions and fry off until the onions are soft. Add the chorizo and cook until it starts to release the red oil.

Add the paprika and ground cumin and stir to cook the spices out.

Add the chickpeas and chopped tomatoes. Stir well, then add the chicken stock.

Cook on a low heat for 20-25 minutes. Just before you're ready to serve, add the spinach and chopped coriander.

A Cool CALIFORNIAN VIBE

Filmore & Union serves up healthy, nutritious food and the relaxed ambience
of San Francisco in its three North Yorkshire restaurants.

Inspired by former wellness clinic owner Adele Ashley's trip to San Francisco and named after her two favourite streets in the city, Filmore & Union brings a touch of Californian cool to North Yorkshire.

Based on healthy eating principles with pure, natural and locally sourced ingredients packed into each dish, Filmore & Union opened for business in 2012. There are now nine restaurants across Yorkshire; York, York Station, Ilkley, Skipton, Wetherby, Beverley, Harrogate, Moortown and Victoria Quarter. They are open for breakfast, lunch, dinner and a delicious Sunday Brunch.

Filmore & Union's marketing manager, Megan Chalk, said: "We really believe a healthy diet is not what you don't eat, but what you do – wholesome food that's pure and natural.

"You wont find refined ingredients in any of our meals and all dishes are cooked fresh from scratch.

"All of our produce is seasonal and delivered fresh from local suppliers. We update the seasonal menu in our restaurants each month with recipes that incorporate seasonal ingredients."

The nutritious ethos is continued in the boutique catering brand that Filmore & Union takes on the road for outside events. Expect to find juices, Gwyneth Paltrow's favourite turmeric latte, wholesome tagines, salads and new seasonal dishes every month and daily changing specials. Filmore & Union is coeliac-accredited and their extensive knowledge of food allergies and intolerances plays an important part in the menu. All cakes are made in their 100% gluten-free bakery in Wetherby, where dairy free and vegan options are also available. The group has already won the Free From eating out award in recognition for their work in this area.

Filmore & Union offer al fresco dining in their rear courtyard herb gardens in Harrogate, Wetherby and Beverley restaurants or out on the terrace at their Ilkley restaurant. The whole restaurant space can also be hired out for events. Not only that but their boutique catering brand can cater for anything from a dinner party at home to a business meeting or a wedding. They also offer a pre-order and collect service - you can order anything from their entertaining at home menu then collect from your nearest Filmore & Union restaurant and take it home with you so you don't have to worry about cooking for that Friday night dinner party.

The range of options at Filmore & Union is always changing with the seasonal produce but you can always find some firm favourites. For breakfast you could go for their poached eggs on toasted rye bread served with hummus, spinach, tomato, mushrooms and pesto or there's the Hot Jack's bagel, paprika roasted chicken with red peppers, homemade guacamole and salad leaves for lunch. And then for dinner you could try their rump steak with spinach, cashew and beetroot hummus and raw veg noodle salad served with baked paprika wedges or a seasonal tagine.

Filmore & Union isn't about denying yourself; most of the restaurants are fully licensed and have stylish cocktail bars that serve wine, beer and refreshing cocktails with gluten-free options available. The atmosphere is relaxed with a signature Californian feel, in restaurants with a rustic but modern décor, including cable knit blankets to wrap up warm when it's cold outside.

Dogs are welcome too, even for dinner. They also offer free WiFi and local newspapers for all customers. It's part of the everyone's welcome vibe you'll find at each Filmore & Union outlet. For more information go to www.filmoreandunion.com.

Filmore & Union
CHICKEN TAGINE WITH DATES AND HONEY

A healthy and hearty Moroccan-influenced dish packed with the flavours of warming spices. Served across all of the Filmore & Union restaurants. It's gluten-free too. Serves 5.

Ingredients

600g chicken

400g red onion, shredded

30g garlic, chopped

5g fresh chillis

7g each of ground cumin, ginger, turmeric and cinnamon

80g dates

55g honey

250g chickpeas

20g coriander

20g spring onions

25ml oil

30ml water

20ml cider vinegar

670ml chicken stock

Method

Preheat the oven to 160°c.

Mix together the fresh chilli, cumin, ginger, turmeric, cinnamon, garlic, oil and water and blend into a paste.

Shred the red onion and lightly fry over a medium heat in a large pan. Add the paste and fry together for a few minutes over a low heat.

Mix the cider vinegar, dates and honey and then add to the paste and red onion mix. Pour in the chicken stock and cook for 30 minutes on a low heat.

Bake chicken in the oven at 160°c for 25-30 minutes until cooked through, ensuring the core temperature of the chicken has reached 80°c.

Add the chickpeas, spring onions and coriander to the base chicken stock mixture and heat on the hob for 5 minutes over a low heat.

Remove the chicken from the oven, dice and add to the base chicken stock mixture.

Garnish with coriander leaves and serve.

The George at Wath

The George at Wath
PANNA COTTA, HONEY, GRANOLA AND STRAWBERRY SOUP

One of the UK's youngest AA Rosette award-winning chefs, local lad Harrison Barraclough has been at the helm at The George at Wath since early 2016. His hallmarks are fresh local produce with a twist, which you'll find on the à la carte and tasting menus. Ingredients are sourced from as close as possible, with herbs and vegetables coming from The George's own kitchen garden. Behind the bar, you'll find local cask ales, a large selection of gins plus an extensive wine list to match with the menus. Serves 6.

Ingredients

For the panna cotta:

250ml double cream

250ml semi-skimmed milk

3 clear gelatine leaves

50g caster sugar

Room temperature water for soaking gelatine

Raw Forest honey, to taste

1 vanilla pod

For the granola:

200g raisins

200g rolled oats

100g sunflower seeds

50g pistachio kernals

100ml Raw Forest honey

For the strawberry soup:

2 punnets of strawberries

500g caster sugar

½ litre of cold water

For garnish:

Strawberries to finish

Handful of baby basil

Handful of pea shoots

250g pistachio kernals

Method

For the panna cotta

Cling film six chefs rings and then cut out the top panel.

Soak the gelatine leaves in room temperature water.

Boil the cream and milk then add the caster sugar and honey to taste. Add a vanilla pod. Whisk in soft gelatine leaves.

Place the rings on a tray. Fill the rings with the panna cotta mixture and place straight into the fridge for a minimum of 3 hours, or until ready to serve.

For the granola

Mix the dry ingredients in a bowl. Heat the honey and add to the dry ingredients.

Put the mix onto a tray and bake in the oven for 20 minutes at 170°c and leave to cool.

When cool, break into pieces using a rolling pin.

For the strawberry soup

Remove the stalks from the strawberries.

Add the sugar and water to a saucepan and boil to just before it sets into a syrup.

Add the strawberries to the loose syrup then place in a food processor and blitz.

For the garnish

Cut the strawberries in quarters.

Blitz the pistachios.

Pick the best pea shoots and baby basil.

To serve

Remove the panna cotta from the ring and place in the middle of your bowl.

Gently warm the strawberry soup.

Place the strawberries and granola across the panna cotta in a single, straight line.

Sprinkle pistachio and garnish with the pea shoots and baby basil.

Serve soup in small jugs to pour around at the table.

Traditional and
MODERN

Two very different dining experiences, flavourful local food and fabulous views are all part of the service at Gisborough Hall Hotel on the edge of the North Yorkshire moors.

Mixing the traditional and the modern in its restaurant, bar and bistro, Gisborough Hall is a country house hotel with a real foodie focus.

Looking out to the Cleveland Hills, the hall was built for Lord Guisborough's Chaloner family in 1857 and is still owned by them today, managed on their behalf by Macdonald Hotels.

"The hotel is very much what the family wanted; it's like coming to stay in a family home," says Kim Yardley, who has been general manager since the hotel opened in 2001.

"The artefacts, pictures and books all belong to the family. Although the hotel has been refurbished, it's kept a traditional but contemporary feel."

Diners enter the dining area past a Victorian walk-in document store that's been transformed into a walk-in whisky and brandy safe. There are two very different dining experiences: the restaurant, Chaloner's, is named after the family and provides elegant dining with beautiful chandeliers, large windows and original features, while the G Bar & Bistro is contemporary and chic, where you can enjoy afternoon tea and seasonal evening meals. Both hotel residents and non-residents are welcome, although it's essential to book.

Head chef Jason Moore, who grew up in Guisborough, specialises in modern British cuisine using locally-sourced ingredients in a menu that changes four times a year and offers different daily specials.

He said: "We use as much local Yorkshire produce as we can – beef, pork and Dales lamb; cheeses, local black pudding and salad.

"We use foraged ingredients as much as possible, such as wild garlic from the estate and even nettles from the wood. People want to know the story of where ingredients came from and where they can get it themselves, and we love to tell everyone about the products we use."

Local doesn't stop at the food. Several of the staff live nearby and have been at Gisborough Hall for many years. Some, like Jason, have returned for a second tour of duty.

Kim said: "We're a big family-orientated business and the friendliest you'll get."

Gisborough Hall Hotel

Gisborough Hall
PLATE OF YORKSHIRE PORK

A superb mix of textures and flavours come together in this dish of tender braised pork cheek fillet wrapped in sage and pancetta, black pudding, apple purée, mashed potatoes, spinach and red wine sauce. Serves 4.

Ingredients

1 pork fillet

100g sliced pancetta

4 x 50g slices black pudding

4 pork cheeks

4 carrots, peeled and chopped

1 leek, chopped

1 onion, chopped

2 cloves garlic

Fresh thyme

Sage

½ tsp ground cumin

2 cooking apples

50g unsalted butter

50g caster sugar

4 baking potatoes

250g spinach

Method

Trim the pork cheeks and place in a pan with the thyme, garlic, one carrot, the leek and onion.

Cover with water and bring to the boil, then simmer for approximately an hour until the cheeks are soft and tender. Remove the cheeks from the stock and set them aside to cool.

Peel, core and chop the apples and place them in a pan with butter and sugar. Cook until the apples are soft, then place in a food processor and blend until smooth.

Trim the pork fillet and place the sage on top. Wrap the fillet in the sliced pancetta and seal in a hot pan with oil to colour all sides. Put the fillet into a preheated oven at 180°c for around 12 minutes or until it's cooked.

Peel and chop the potatoes and place in a pan with salted water. Bring to the boil, cook until soft then drain and mash with a knob of butter and seasoning.

Put the remaining peeled and chopped carrots in a pan with the ground cumin and bring to the boil. Cook until soft, then whizz the carrots in a blender with a knob of butter. Add a splash of the cooking water to make a purée.

Wash the spinach and wilt in a pan with a knob of butter.

Heat up your black pudding in a dry frying pan, plate up and enjoy.

Entente
CORDIALE

Eating at The Grange Hotel fuses French cuisine with local ingredients in an elegant setting.

Set in a stunning Regency townhouse in York, The Grange Hotel was built in 1829 and during World War II, the building housed women working for the war effort. Today, echoes of the building's past can be glimpsed when you sit down for a meal or enjoy afternoon tea.

The two-rosette Ivy Brasserie in the vaulted cellars was once an air raid shelter and now has a contemporary feel, but the Regency heritage is obvious in the Morning Room, Library and Drawing Room which can be booked for private parties, weddings and christenings.

A hotel since 1990, The Grange majors in French cuisine with a Yorkshire twist.

Head chef, Will Nicol, who trained in the UK and across the channel said "We use Yorkshire produce whenever possible, making the majority of dishes on site."

Suppliers are all small companies that Will has worked with for many years, including local butchers, fishmongers and artisan cheese suppliers. He promotes seasonal flavours in the frequently changing menus and specials. Yorkshire rhubarb, black pudding, monkfish wrapped in cured ham are popular with diners and Whitby crab cakes are a year round staple.

"Local produce is paramount, but combining these ingredients with those from further afield is also important. The tartiflette for example, a traditional French dish, is made with local charcuterie, heritage potatoes and Reblochon cheese."

At night, the Ivy Brasserie's open brickwork is lit by candles and dimmed industrial lighting, whilst the upstairs dining areas retain their early 19th century feel, enhanced by the rare racing silks on loan from York Racecourse.

Helen Smith, who manages sales and marketing, said: "It's a bit two-tone – upstairs is quite traditional while the brasserie is quirky and modern."

The Grange Hotel

IVY BRASSERIE

The Grange Hotel
YORKSHIRE CURD TART

They'll be queuing out of your kitchen door for second helpings of
The Grange Hotel's take on this traditional Yorkshire tea time treat.

Ingredients

For the pastry:

2 eggs

100g sugar

250g margarine

400g plain flour

Baking beans for blind baking

For the filling:

100g caster sugar

450g curd cheese

4 eggs

4 egg yolks

2 lemons, zest only

50g butter, melted

100g currants

Freshly grated nutmeg

Method

For the pastry

Preheat the oven to 160^0c.

Crumb together the flour and the margarine. In a separate bowl, whisk together the eggs and sugar.

Gradually add the egg mix to the flour mix until a dough is formed but don't over-work the pastry.

When the dough is formed, wrap the pastry in cling film and chill for 30 minutes. Then lightly flour your rolling pin and surface and roll out the pastry to a 30cm circle.

Roll the pastry around the rolling pin and ease it into a grease fluted loose based tart tin. Press it into the base lightly with your fingers.

Line the pastry with baking paper and fill with baking beans. Bake for 7 minutes, then remove the baking beans and bake for a further 7 minutes.

Put the pastry to one side to cool.

For the filling

Preheat the oven to 180^0c.

Beat the sugar and curd together and mix until smooth, then beat in the eggs, egg yolks and lemon zest.

When these are well combined, add the melted butter and currants. Pour into the tart case and grate fresh nutmeg over top.

Bake for 20 minutes or until the mixture has set.

Homecooked HERITAGE

Sitting in the shadow of York Minister, Grays Court offers history aplenty and menu packed with Yorkshire ingredients.

Dining at Grays Court, a hidden gem in the heart of historic York, puts you in elevated company.

James I once ate here and knighted eight noblemen in one night, and the Grade I listed building in the shadow of York Minister once belonged to the Duke of Somerset, whose sister Jane Seymour was Henry VIII's favourite wife. It was also visited by anti-slavery campaigner William Wilberforce, and was owned for a long time by the Gray family, from whom it takes its name.

"We're adding our name to the list," says Rhiannon Heraty, whose family bought the run-down building in 2005 and spent five years turning it into a restaurant, wedding, conference and banqueting venue and boutique hotel.

"My mum Helen had run B&Bs for years but we'd never had a hotel or listed building. We sold everything and jumped in at the deep end."

Grays Court restaurant has a "simple, elegant and calming" ambience, Rhiannon says, and a modern British menu that concentrates on fresh Yorkshire flavours. Local food is used for the mix of seafood, red meat and vegetarian options, which constantly evolve with the seasons. There's also a fantastic afternoon tea selection, including a Champagne option.

Rhiannon said: "It's locally sourced and nice and simple; food that speaks for itself – good Yorkshire fare but polished to a high restaurant standard. We use Whitby crab, local meats and bread from just around the corner."

The restaurant attracts a real variety of diners, from young couples choosing it as a venue for their proposal and then their wedding, to students, lecturers and tourists. Many of the visitors are bewitched by the building's 900-year heritage and the character that goes with it, including the huge 85ft by 12ft Long Gallery, Jacobean oak interiors and beautiful Georgian fireplaces.

"Grays Court is a family run business, we want people to immerse themselves in the history of the building whilst still feeling comfortable, relaxed and at home," adds Rhiannon.

Grays Court

FILLET OF WOOLPOTS FARM BEEF AND CRISPY CHEEK, LITTLE OXTAIL PIE, CELERIAC PURÉE, BOULANGÈRE POTATOES AND MADEIRA JUS

Yorkshire ingredients slow cooked with a French twist. Serves 2.

Ingredients

2 x 113g (4oz) fillet steak

1 beef cheek

1kg oxtail

1 bottle red wine

1 litre good quality beef stock

100ml Madeira wine

1 sprig thyme

1kg potatoes, half cooked and mashed and half for the Boulangère potatoes

500g carrots, diced

1 celeriac

1 stalk celery

2 onions

50g baby spinach

250g butter

100ml double cream

50g breadcrumbs

Salt and pepper

Method

For the beef

Roll the fillet steak in cling film and refrigerate until needed.

Sear the beef cheek in a frying pan and then braise in the oven at 160˚c, with enough red wine to just cover the meat, for 2-3 hours until falling apart.

Once cooled, shred the meat, season and mix with a of the little mashed potato. Form into two croquette shapes and roll in breadcrumbs. Refrigerate until needed.

For the little oxtail pie

Sear outside of the oxtail then braise with red wine, the sprig of thyme, diced carrots, celery and one of the onions for 3-4 hours at 160˚c, until the meat is falling off the bone. Separate the meat from the bone and discard the bone.

In a pan, reduce the braising liquid by two-thirds, then mix in the oxtail meat, braised carrots, celery and onion. Season to taste.

Place in two small ramekins and pipe mashed potato on top, then refrigerate until needed

For the celeriac purée

Remove outer skin from the celeriac and slice into 2cm thick pieces. Boil until soft then place in food processor with a little of the cooking water and blend until smooth. Mix in the double cream and season.

For the Boulangère potatoes

Thinly slice the potatoes and the second onion into an ovenproof dish, add the butter and cover with beef stock. Cook very slowly in the oven on a low heat. In the restaurant, we cook these the day before so we can press them in the fridge to be cut into any shape we want.

For the Madeira jus

Reduce the remaining beef stock to a jus then add 100ml of Madeira and reduce again until it coats the back of a spoon.

To serve

Place the Boulangère potatoes and mini oxtail pie in oven at 200˚c for 15 minutes. Deep fry the ox cheek croquettes and fry the fillet steak to your requirements.

In saucepans, heat the celeriac purée and Madeira jus. Wilt the baby spinach with butter.

Swipe the purée onto the plates, place the Boulangère potatoes at top of the purée and put the spinach off-centre. Place the oxtail pie at end of the purée, and a croquette and the fillet steak on top of the spinach. Drizzle with Madeira jus.

Haxby Bakehouse
CLASSIC WHITE SOURDOUGH

Artisan bread made with traditional slow fermentation techniques and organic flours is the hallmark of Haxby Bakehouse in Haxby near York that has been run by husband and wife team Phil and Tina Clayton since 2008. The bakehouse's deli sells a superb selection of local cheeses, pâtés, plus imported cured meats and home baked hams and roasted beef cooked on the premises to partner perfectly with the fresh bread. Phil also runs full day baking courses where you can discover tips and techniques for making your own real bread at home.
Makes 1 large 800g or 2 small 400g loaves.

Ingredients

475g organic strong white bread flour

25g organic dark rye flour

150g wheat sourdough starter (visit our website for instructions how to create your own starter or pop in to pick some up for free)

350g water

10g salt

Method

Depending on your skill level, the loaves can either be formed and proved in baskets or shaped and placed into bread tins. Bread tins won't give the characteristic open crumb of a sourdough but you will get a great tasting sandwich loaf.

Your sourdough starter will need to be fed 12-16 hours beforehand so it's nice and active.

Weigh water into a bowl and add the sourdough starter. This should be bubbly and float on the water.

Add both flours and incorporate until there's no dry flour left. We're not looking for a smooth dough yet. Cover the bowl and leave for 30 minutes.

Add the salt and fully incorporate into the dough. Knead for 3-4 minutes. The dough will be sticky, but don't worry and try not to add any extra flour. Embrace the stickiness.

Place the dough into a clean lightly oiled bowl and cover. The dough needs to bulk prove for 2 hours. During this time, you need to fold it three times at half-hourly intervals.

To fold, work around the dough stretching the sides into the middle, on the second time around you'll feel the dough starting to resist. Twice round is great, we're starting to put strength into the dough.

After 2 hours and three folds, shape the dough into a ball and divide if you're making two small loaves. Rest the dough for 5 minutes then shape as tightly as you can. Place into a floured proving basket or tins and leave for 1½-2 hours.

Preheat a pizza stone or heavy tray in a 220°c oven.

Flour a board and tip out the loaf, slash with a knife and slide onto the oven stone. If you're using tins, slash the surface and place on the tray/stone. Spray the sides of the oven with water from a garden squirter.

Bake for 35-40 minutes for a large loaf or 30-35 minutes for smaller ones. We like to give our loaves a "bold" bake. Colour equals flavour. Allow to cool and enjoy.

Underneath THE ARCHES

Step below the streets of Skipton into Le Caveau Restaurant for a truly arresting experience.

Literally meaning a cave or vault, Le Caveau Restaurant is hidden away in a subterranean location beneath the cobbled High Street in Skipton.

Once you've had a taste of chef-owner Mark Byron's fantastic Yorkshire fare, you may not want to leave. But at least you have the choice, unlike the former visitors to this 16th century building which was once the local jail. It still retains the barrel vaulted ceilings, original beams and stonework – and maybe some previous inmates.

"Some people say they feel a bit of a presence sat at certain tables," says Mark, who is an avowed non-believer in ghostly guests.

But he is a big believer in the local produce that goes in creating the modern British and European menus that change six times. Frequent new specials reflect the availability of fresh ingredients, including game from the moors.

Mark said: "I have three friends who are gamekeepers on local shoots so we get game direct from the estates and there are two chaps who supply local venison for us.

"I shoot myself, so the pigeons and rabbits I get myself. Everything is supplied in feather, straight off the moors and into our kitchen.

"As soon as 12 August hits, we start getting the grouse in. We sell a lot more grouse – it was a specialist thing, but in the last five or six years, the amount of people willing to try things has gone through the roof."

Mark's adventurous menu also extends to locally sourced goat, which goes into a hugely popular Goan curry. Fish comes from Fleetwood – "we're closer to the west coast than the east," explains Mark.

He and wife Esther have been at the helm since 2014 and Le Caveau holds a special place in their hearts.

"My wife brought me here on our second date and we became regular customers from there on," said Mark.

"When I got itchy feet, I asked the owner about taking over. He was ready to retire and said 'if you want to have a talk about it …'

"What we do is good honest cooking, but we like to put a nice bit of flair on it, and it's as local as you can get."

Le Caveau

Le Caveau
SLOW COOKED YORKSHIRE RABBIT IN CIDER

A taste of wild Yorkshire served with summer vegetables and liver dumplings.
Serves 4.

Ingredients

For the rabbit:

2 rabbits, jointed

2 candy beetroot

2 sticks celery

1 large white onion

2 cloves garlic

2 large carrots

250g garden peas

1 cabbage (hispi or savoy)

2 sprigs mint

2 sprigs thyme

2 sprigs dill

2 sprigs flat leaf parsley

500ml cider

1 litre chicken stock

Plain flour for dusting

For the dumplings:

2 rabbit livers

200g self-raising flour

100g beef suet

Salt and pepper to taste

Water to bind

Method

For the rabbit

Dust the rabbit with the flour and fry until golden, then transfer to an ovenproof dish or pan.

Dice the onion, celery and carrot and mince the garlic, then fry until softened but without colour. Transfer to the dish with the rabbit.

Tie half the herbs together and place in with the rabbit. Pour in the cider and chicken stock, then cover the dish and cook in the oven at 160°c for approximately 2 hours.

Whilst the rabbit is cooking, cook the beetroot in boiling salted water until tender then cool, peel and dice into 1cm cubes.

Shred the cabbage and boil with the peas for one minute in salted water. Refresh in iced water to retain the colours.

Chop the remaining herbs and set to one side.

For the dumplings

Blend together the flour, suet, rabbit livers and salt and pepper in a food processor. It should make a sticky paste but if it's too dry, add a little water, and if too wet more flour can be added.

Once the rabbit is cooked, place the dish or pan on the stove and bring to a simmer. Spoon in the dumpling mixture, allowing space to expand, then cover and cook for four minutes, while the dumplings puff up.

Add the beetroot, peas, cabbage and the remaining herbs and cook for another minute before serving.

Locally LOCKWOODS

With heritage fruit and vegetables from a nearby museum garden and constantly evolving menus, Ripon's Lockwoods Restaurant has the local and seasonal approach nailed.

It has been over a decade since Lockwoods opened its doors in one of the country's smallest cities, Ripon, and in this time it has become a much loved part of the North Yorkshire culinary scene.

The restaurant is very much the creation of self-taught chef and restaurateur Matthew Lockwood, who took an empty building and transformed it into an eatery voted Best Restaurant in the North East 2016 by the Good Food Guide.

"I wanted to create a restaurant that everyone could enjoy, whether for brunch, lunch or dinner," said Matthew.

The team at Lockwoods has worked hard to create a relaxed, friendly place where the customer is always put first – right down to the restaurant's mantra of "just ask, if we have it, and we can make it, we will."

"The little things are so important. We create good food and work hard to ensure our service and surroundings match this and are the best they can be." Matthew continued.

The food is a grown up affair with dishes like pan-fried sea bream with chorizo and homemade potato gnocchi to 45-day dry aged steak from Farmison & Co down the road, and menus change every few weeks to reflect the best of local and seasonal produce. Never one to rest on its laurels, Lockwoods produces its own black pudding, cures its own meats and makes its own chutneys.

During the summer months, Matthew and his team have a beneficial relationship with the nearby Workhouse Museum's garden, using their heritage herbs, vegetables and salad to create an inspiring summer menu, from field to fork in a couple of hours!

Matthew said: "The museum is 200 yards away and we use the best produce grown over the summer, delivered fresh each morning and on the menu for lunchtime."

Matthew says that the sustainable aspect of eating is something that has become increasingly important to diners.

"Customers are now so accustomed to influences from all over the world, so the team here take European and world influences to create interesting dishes, but always with local and seasonal produce and a firm nod to our Yorkshire roots."

As for the restaurant's interior, its light and airy during the day and warm and welcoming in the evening with thick fur throws, dark wood tables and little cubbyholes to tuck yourself away in at the bar. Gentle lighting and trees growing out of the floor add to its charm, and walls adorned with paintings by a local artist. It's a blend of traditional and contemporary that makes everyone feel at home in its busy and buzzing atmosphere, as smartly dressed staff ensure that you get just what you need from your dining out experience.

Lockwoods Restaurant

LOCKWOODS

BRUNCH   LUNCH   DINNER   COCKTAILS

WINNER!
RESTAURANT OF T
YEAR → NORTH-E
2016
WE DID IT

Waitrose
GOOD FOOD
GUIDE
2016

THANK YOU TO EVERYONE WHO VOTE
FLAVOUR TO SAVOUR – THAT'S LOCK
AT LOCKWOODS, WE MAKE IT FRESH

Lockwoods Restaurant

YORKSHIRE PORK CURED IN SMOKED PAPRIKA, YOUNG GREEN VEGETABLES, JERSEY ROYALS AND ROAST HAZELNUT DRESSING

This is a fabulous light dish that can be cooked in the kitchen or even better on the barbeque, which gives the pork even more smoky flavours for the perfect taste of summer. This dish also uses the fantastic peas, broad beans and asparagus that are around in summer, alongside lots of soft herbs to give the dish a lovely lightness. The smoked paprika from Spain brings to mind summer holidays on the continent. Serves 4.

Ingredients

For the pork:

4 pork fillets, trimmed

3 tbsp sea salt

2 tbsp caster sugar

1 tbsp smoked paprika

For the roast hazelnut dressing:

50g roast hazelnuts

1 tbsp shallots, finely chopped

1 clove garlic, finely chopped

50ml hazelnut oil

1 tsp red wine vinegar

For the salad:

4 or 5 small cooked Jersey Royals

200g fresh peas, podded and blanched

200g broad beans, skinned and blanched

4 asparagus spears, blanched

1 bunch baby watercress

Handful of fresh chives and mint, chopped

Olive oil

Red wine vinegar

Method

For the pork

Mix together the salt, sugar and smoked paprika and rub it into the pork. Marinate for four hours then wash off the mix.

Pan fry the pork or cook on the barbeque, turning frequently until the fillets are caramelised all over. This should take approximately 10-12 minutes.

Let the pork rest.

For the dressing

Put all the ingredients apart from the oil in a blender and whizz together while slowly adding the oil. Season with salt and pepper.

To serve

Just before serving, combine all the vegetables and herbs and lightly mix together with olive oil and vinegar.

Place the freshly mixed salad in a warm bowl, lay slices of pork over the top and drizzle with the roasted hazelnut dressing.

Made In MALTON

Malton Food Lovers Festival director and passionate foodie Tom Naylor-Leyland shares his vision for Yorkshire's food capital.

I think the reason I love Malton is that at its heart it's still very much a working town: flat-capped farmers at livestock sales; young jockeys grabbing lunch between a ride; half a pig being carried into the butcher's or a crate of shiny crabs going into the fishmonger. There's a realness to Malton, old-fashioned, charming, but living and breathing too.

My vision was to take the incredible local produce – game, shellfish, rare breed meat, cheese, beer, baking and more – and celebrate it right here in Yorkshire.

I'm proud that today you can taste your way around town, eating delicious dishes, buying the famous local produce and learning how to cook it at Malton Cookery School.

Malton still has traditional butchers, bakers and grocers, which is quite unusual for a small town these days. Now it also produces its own food and drink, much of it at Talbot Yard Food Court.

Based in a former coaching yard, the food court is a hive of activity where you'll find Made in Malton food producers making the finest artisan food and have the opportunity to learn more about their crafts, as well as buy some great ingredients to take home.

Talbot Yard Food Court is a stop on our Malton Food Tour, and I get a thrill knowing visitors can see bread baked, beer brewed and coffee roasted. You can even see butter hand churned and fresh pasta made too.

People in Malton always have time to talk, and the food tour of our Made in Malton producers is perfect for a chat. I adore finding out from Michelle at Groovy Moo which gelato is this week's favourite or from Aldo which ravioli he's making that day.

As Malton has become a tourist destination, I'm so excited that people from all across the UK are deciding to spend more of their holidays here.

Whether it's our traditional food shops, Made in Malton producers, food tour, markets, festivals, cookery school or restaurants, I am sure you and your family will find something to enjoy, nibble or take home.

For me it's the quintessential Yorkshire market town, but then I am a bit biased…

Hope to meet you in Malton soon!

Tom Naylor-Leyland, Malton Food Lovers Festival Director (that's me in the cow apron pulling a pint)

Amazing Ice Cream
REAL BREAD AND FRESH COFFEE

Artisan food businesses making products with love and care is the essence of the Talbot Yard Food Court experience in Malton.

Groovy Moo Gelato

Family-run Groovy Moo really is something special: Italian-style gelato ice cream crafted by Michelle Walker, her son Ashley Smith and daughter Amy Linford.

"My son was taught to make gelato by a professor from the Carpigiani Gelato University in Bologna and we use the Italian method of balancing recipes," says Michelle.

"Every one is done to a different formulation. It's lower in fat and sugar and smoother and warmer on the palate."

Milk comes from St Quintin's Creamery at Harpham and fresh in-season fruit from the local greengrocer, so the flavours change constantly.

Groovy Moo was born out of tragedy. Michelle gave up her previous soft ice cream making business in Bridlington to care for her husband, who had terminal cancer.

She said: "My husband was born and bred in Malton. He said: 'I hope the people in Malton see what I saw in you.'

"You throw yourself into something – you don't forget, but you stand stronger. As a family, we've dug deep and created something that people can't get enough of."

Roost Coffee & Roastery

Roost Coffee & Roastery is an independent, family run business consisting of David and Ruth and their daughters Erin and Betsy. They hand roast small batches of coffee beans from a beautifully converted carriage house in Talbot Yard, Malton. Roost delivers the freshest coffee possible by roasting green beans that go out to customers, including coffee shops, restaurants and hotels, within seven days of each roast. For the Roost team though, forging strong relationships with its customers is just as important as great coffee.

While supplying speciality coffee beans to wholesale and retail customers, they also offer coffee lovers the opportunity to visit the roastery and try out a variety of beans at their in-house espresso bar. This is open to the public, Wednesdays to Saturdays, 10am – 2pm.

Roost offers two espresso blends, Roost Espresso, a medium roast ideal for breakfast and daytime drinking, and Tonto Espresso, a darker roasted bean great for after lunch or dinner. They also roast several single origin coffees and a Swiss Water Decaf, all roasted on their environmentally friendly Diedrich IR12 roaster.

David said: "The single origin coffee changes every couple of months; it's speciality coffee that's traceable from farms, single estates and cooperatives. This provides individual amazing tastes and aromas not usually found in your average cup"

The business is also the only one in the North of England to work with Rocket Espresso Milano coffee machines, noted as one of the best in Europe.

Bluebird Bakery

Bluebird Bakery began life in the kitchen of Al and Nicky Kippax's terraced house. The company quickly outgrew its humble beginnings and now makes 'real bread', pastries, focaccia and sweeter treats at Talbot Yard food court in central Malton.

The bakery uses traditional techniques with wild yeast and organic flour to create hand-moulded bread which carries the 'loaf mark' of the Real Bread Campaign, to show it meets real bread criteria.

Nicky said: "Real bread calls for long-fermentation methods and can take up to 48 hours to make. Our bread uses the simplest ingredients – flour, water and a little salt; no additives or preservatives – but it's full of flavour."

Ex-chef Al grew an appetite for bread-making during a course in Scotland. The family then moved from London and decided to bring their passion for proper bread to North Yorkshire.

Originally hand-delivering goods to friends, local shops and farmers markets, Bluebird Bakery now supplies delis, restaurants and bars from its Malton bakery and York shop on Little Shambles.

Demand has grown so much that Al has now employed two other bakers to help make bread throughout the night.

Traditional Butchery
HAND-CHURNED BUTTER & HOMEMADE PASTA

Handmade Malton goodies have really put the town on the foodies' must-visit map.

Food 2 Remember

Paul Potts has been butchering for more than 30 years but Food 2 Remember is much more than meat.

The business, which is a specialist in 28-day dry aged steaks from pedigree Hereford cattle sourced from within a 15-mile radius, moved from a van delivery service into the Talbot Yard Food Court in late 2015.

Paul said: "We were a little hidden secret but a lot of people are now finding us. Our motto is 'always something different'."

Food 2 Remember's pork is free-range, the lamb is flavourful hogget and the chicken is herb fed, and according to Paul's customers it's "the best around".

The shop makes its own 95 percent meat sausages, with flavours changing to reflect the seasons such as pork and wild garlic and pork and asparagus.

Specially-made ready meals and a fish counter creating delicacies like haddock Scotch eggs made from a mouth watering combination of smoked haddock, leeks and cheddar, and paella fishcakes, are part of the mix along with a wide range of gluten-free products.

Paul, whose daughter Betsie, 19, and son Kieran, 16, also help out, said: "I'm a cook as well as a butcher. People come in to ask for luxury pies and ready meals."

With a bit of guidance on what you want, Paul will go away and create a special dish for you to take home. It certainly is food you'll remember.

ButterBees of Malton

"People say it's almost like clotted cream," says Stephen Briden-Kenny of the handcrafted butter that he and wife Lucy make at ButterBees in Malton Market Street.

The couple gave up high pressure careers – Stephen in food production safety and Lucy in law – to move to Malton to make real Yorkshire butter using a churn they designed themselves.

ButterBees butter takes 45 minutes to an hour to make by hand, using high-welfare organic cream.

"The cows are really well-looked after and they are kept at pasture for as long as possible," says Stephen.

"They have memory foam mattresses, massages and a self-milking machine."

The Briden-Kennys are the only people commercially making hand-churned butter north of the Watford Gap. They sell through the parlour in Malton, online and to retail customers including farm shops, delis, cafés and hotels. Each bar of butter is with the buyer within 24 hours of being made.

"Malton is a really foodie town, and we wanted to be in a world where we were working for ourselves and creating things that people like to eat" said Stephen.

Passione Della Pasta

Aldo Valerio swapped careers from cheese making to pasta making a decade ago and now sells his unique homemade pastas and sauces from Talbot Yard Food Court.

Aldo's parents arrived in the UK from southern Italy in the 1950s and began producing Italian cheeses and meat products as well as importing Italian foods and wines they'd known at home. Now their son creates a huge choice of filled and plain pastas under the Passione Della Pasta – passion for pasta – brand. They're all made from local free-range eggs and the best Italian durum wheat flour and have the authentic taste you'd expect from a real artisan food producer.

Visitors can see pasta making in action and take home traditional Italian favourites or new spins on pasta, such as the Yorkshire game ravioli.

Aldo said: "The raviolis are popular, and all the fillings come from local suppliers. There are so many you can do."

Aldo also produces four different sauces to perfectly complement the pasta to give you a real taste of Italy – and Yorkshire – at home.

Made With LOVE

Masons Yorkshire Gin is a small batch craft gin, created with love and care by gin connoisseurs Karl and Cathy Mason.

The creation of Masons Yorkshire Gin was truly a labour of love – Karl and Cathy Mason's love of gin.

It all started with a Facebook page where the Masons and their friends would share pictures of themselves enjoying a G&T on a Friday night. The page became so popular, it soon had 10,000 followers and attracted the attention of gin manufacturers. They started sending samples for the Masons to test and share pictures on the page.

Karl said: "I was having one that had been sent to me and I said to Cathy: 'There's nothing new about this gin. It tastes the same old; I bet I could do better'.

"And she said: 'Why don't you?'"

The seed was planted. Karl, who had no experience in distilling – "I hadn't even worked in a bar" – and Cathy set out on months of research, recipe testing and finding a distiller to make the first batches. The first bottles were produced in 2012 and Masons Yorkshire Gin drinkers can now be found in Italy and Australia.

Today, the spirit is made in Bedale in the Masons' own 300-litre copper still named Steve, with the addition of a secret mixture of botanicals including juniper, coriander, bay leaf, lime and cardamom. As well as the original recipe, Masons also comes in Yorkshire Tea and Lavender varieties. But they all have the same spirit.

"I call it the Yorkshire spirit, because it's a little bit no nonsense and it packs a punch," says Karl.

"There's also the quality; when you distil, you get the heads, tails and heart. You only bottle the heart and we collect a smaller heart than other people, and throw away more."

The Masons quit their previous careers to concentrate on gin – Karl in publishing and Cathy as a special educational needs teacher. Ultimately, they want a gin visitor centre at their distillery site.

"My ambition is to have a brown tourist sign," says Karl. "We're committed to Bedale. We want to be known as the distilling centre of Yorkshire.

"There is a gin boom at the moment. The bulk of people joining it have a lot of money and want to cash in." Karl adds. "We started with no money and for the right reasons – an absolute love of gin."

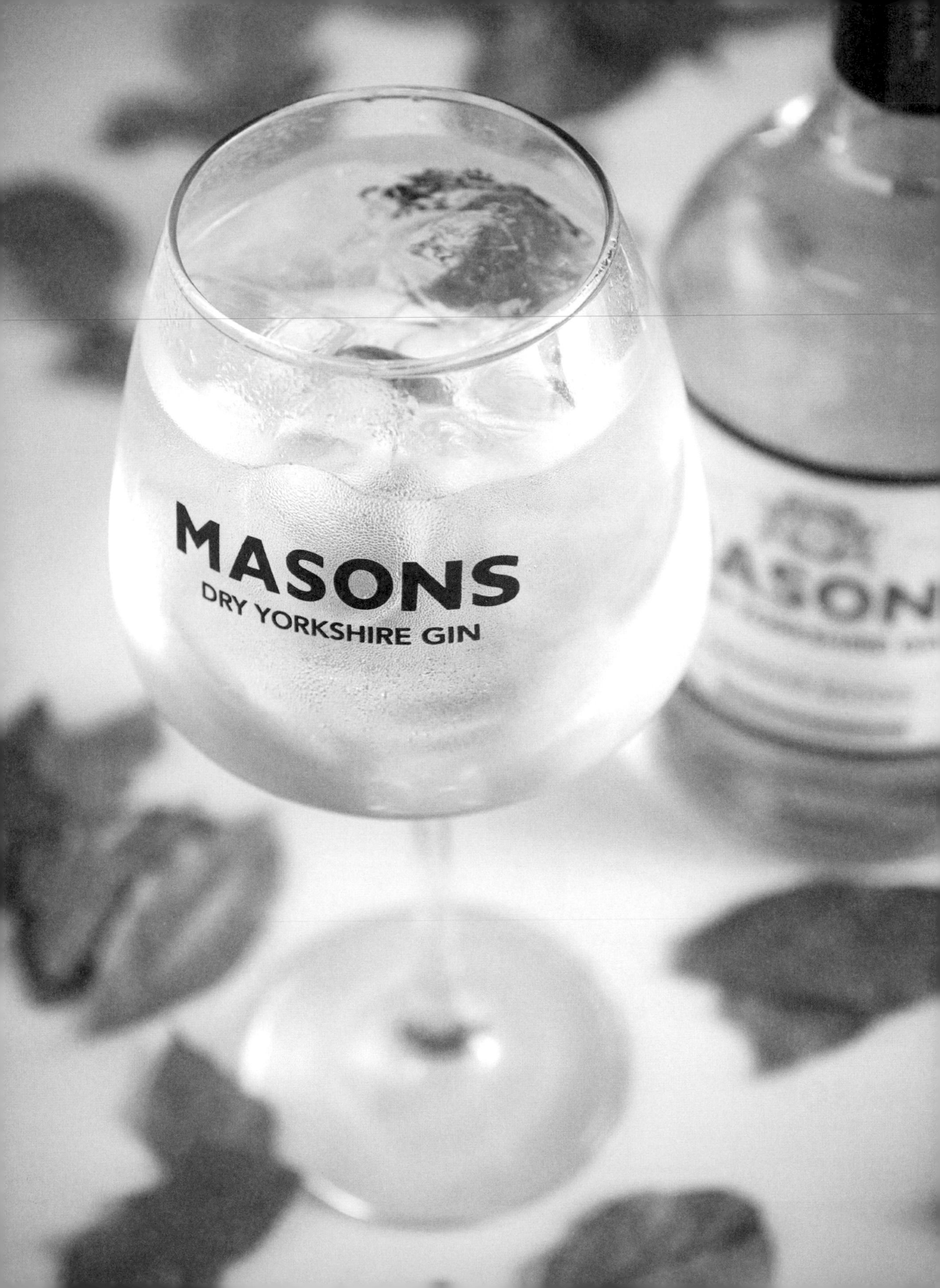
MASONS
DRY YORKSHIRE GIN

Masons Gin
G&T PURE AND SIMPLE

Gin and tonic is THE classic way to serve gin. It's so simple but such an easy drink to serve badly – no ice, no garnish, poor tonic – most bars have in the past been guilty of at least one of these sins.

Ingredients

Masons Gin

Ice

Tonic Water

Your choice of garnish

Method

At Masons we are passionate about serving gin and tonic properly. These are the Masons Gin top tips to get the most out of your drink:

1. Use lots of ice - more ice stops the ice melting.

2. Use good quality tonic water; it's approximately three-quarters of your drink, so why ruin a good gin with poor tonic?

3. Get your garnish right. Some people prefer lime, others lemon but it's not that simple Garnishes should be chosen according to what compliments the botanicals in your gin.

For example, orange compliments the cardamom in our original gin; lemon and tea are a proven flavour combination, so we garnish our tea edition with it and the sweet floral nature of lavender needs the sharpness of lime to balance it.

Experiment and play around with your garnishes. It affects the 'nose' of your drink, which is something you experience before you even taste it. Never underestimate the power of the garnish.

For the perfect Masons Gin, we serve our drinks with a premium tonic such as Fevertree or Fentimans.

These are our garnish suggestions to get the most out of your Masons Gin:

Original edition

Mrs Mason likes it with orange zest and Mr Mason likes it with pink grapefruit zest and cracked black pepper.

Tea edition

Garnish with lemon zest.

Lavender edition

Garnish with lime zest or muddled rhubarb.

Delicious Dining and
CREATIVE CATERING

Regional food is the star of the show at no8's flagship bistro,
cafés and catering business in York.

Seasonal and local produce are at the heart of everything that the no8 team do. They are big believers in creating delicious dishes from the very best fresh produce.

Starting out with a bistro at no8 Gillygate, they also now have a tea room at the Merchant Adventurers' Hall, a café at the York Art Gallery and the Pavilion Pop Up – Museum Gardens and a catering business specialising in 'rustic feasts' for weddings and events.

"We use the Yorkshire Forager, who comes in with fresh, seasonal foraged goods – and we select what we like and transform them into a new menu every six weeks," says Matthew Hyde, who has been a chef for 15 years in some of Yorkshire's best restaurants.

Matthew and wife Ashley Hyde, a former event manager, are directors in the no8 team started in 2002 by self-taught patron chef Chris Pragnell and previous owner Martin Gore. The three together now manage the business with a strong set of core values originating from its roots and employ a dedicated team of 34 people in York.

A strong food ethos runs through each of the venues, with the flagship bistro serving up some of no8's more experimental

dishes. Each shares a menu packed with local ingredients, with Yorkshire suppliers playing a key role.

Ashley said: "It's all homemade and locally sourced, and we work with the community. We use Holgate Windmill flour in our bread and honey comes from Bootham just across the street.

"We work in conjunction with the Fruity Kitchen to make our own brown sauce and tomato ketchup that customers can enjoy with their breakfast or buy and use at home."

Meat, fish, cheese and vegetables all come from nearby suppliers and even the flowers on the table are sourced from Ducks and Daffodils in York.

no8 has a strong base of regulars, who get to taste new recipes and are asked to provide feedback when the team is revamping the seasonal menus, and it's also popular with tourists visiting the city.

Ashley, who was named the York Press Awards Young Entrepreneur of the Year 2015, said: "Our motto is delicious dining and creative catering in the heart of Yorkshire.

"We absolutely love what we do."

no8 bistro

THRILLER IN VANILLA SOURDOUGH BREAD

Made using Holgate Windmill Flour, the trick to sourdough is patience
and care, but if you can bake bread you'll never go hungry.
Makes one loaf (and starter for many more).

Ingredients

For the sourdough starter:

150g Holgate Windmill wholemeal flour

100ml Mrs Simpson's Thriller in Vanilla porter beer

For the loaf:

500g strong white flour

300g sourdough starter

100ml vanilla porter

150ml tepid water

20g brown sugar

15g salt

Olive oil for kneading

Method

For the sourdough starter

To make the sourdough starter, we mix the flour and porter beer and leave in a Kilner jar for four days to ferment. After that, we feed the starter daily with 80ml of water and 130g wholemeal flour.

You can start to make bread from this after a week.

To make the sourdough loaf

Combine the flour, starter, salt, and sugar in large mixing bowl. Add the tepid water and vanilla porter slowly whilst mixing. Transfer to a food processor or mixer and mix on a high setting for 2 minutes.

Remove the dough and knead for 10 minutes with a little oil.

Place the dough in lightly oiled bowl, cover with cling film and leave to prove for 4-5 hours.

Take out of the bowl and knead again for 2 minutes, then place in a floured bowl or banneton basket. Leave to rise again for 4-6 hours - the longer the prove, the better the bread.

Preheat the oven to 220°c: a high heat to get a good rise and crusty top.

Turn out the bread onto baking tray lined with parchment paper and bake for 30 minutes, then reduce the oven temperature to 180°c for 15-20 minutes.

Cool on wire rack, break bread and enjoy!

PHEASANT KIEV WITH WILD GARLIC, HAZELNUTS AND PEA CUSTARD

A dish that brings together game and foraged ingredients for a flavourful alternative to the usual chicken Kiev. Serves 4.

Ingredients

For the wild garlic hazelnut butter:

100g wild garlic

200g salted butter

10g hazelnuts, chopped

For the Kiev's:

4 pheasant breasts, skin removed

150g seasoned plain flour

180g Panko breadcrumbs

20g hazelnuts, blitzed

2 free-range eggs, whisked with a little water

Vegetable oil, for shallow frying

For the pea custard:

5 large free-range egg yolks

350g peas, blanched and puréed

15g sugar

50ml double cream

Pinch nutmeg

Method

For the wild garlic butter

Blanch the wild garlic for a few seconds in simmering water, then place in ice cold water and squeeze dry. Mix with soft butter and blend, then stir in the chopped hazelnuts.

Pipe the butter on top of the cling film, roll up and freeze.

For the Kiev's

Make an incision on the underside of the pheasant breast underneath the tenderloin. Insert a disc of the frozen garlic butter.

Cover the incision tightly then cover the breasts in the flour, eggs, then a mixture of the blitzed hazelnuts and breadcrumbs.

Seal the Kiev's in a hot pan with vegetable oil until golden brown on both sides. Cook in the oven for 12 minutes at 180°c.

For the pea custard

Whisk the sugar and egg yolks together in bowl, whilst bringing the cream to the simmer. When the cream is hot, pour over the egg yolks and sugar, then mix in the pea purée.

Pour the mixture into a saucepan, season and add nutmeg. Cook on low heat until it coats the back of a spoon, pass through a sieve and chill.

To serve:

Serve the Kiev and pea custard on top of some crushed peas, shelled broad beans and ice lettuce (not iceberg).

Country
COMFORTS

Quality Yorkshire ingredients are the stars of the show at
The Pheasant country hotel in Harome.

"Less is more" is the culinary philosophy of Peter Neville, head chef and director of The Pheasant Hotel at Harome, who draws inspiration – and ingredients – from the surrounding countryside.

Peter worked under Andrew Pern at The Star in Harome and at Hibiscus in London with Claude Bosi before taking the reins at The Pheasant in 2009. Two years later, his approach earned the 2011 Yorkshire Life Restaurant of the Year accolade.

"My style is very elegant, fine dining, light and refreshing dishes," says Peter. "It's all about finding quality ingredients and getting them through the door. There's a little bit of a wild food element in there; we are literally on the doorstep of the countryside.

"I can see the area where wild garlic grows and we use things that are around us. It's the same with the suppliers – finding the best suppliers in the area and the best food we can."

For Peter, that means North Yorkshire produce wherever possible, and because Harome is at the heart of the farming community, access to fresh ingredients is easy. He describes the local meat and vegetables as "absolutely exceptional" and has built relationships with local suppliers. "They've been doing it for years and there's a real trust element between supplier and chef that I've never seen anywhere else," he said.

Converted into a country hotel from a combination of a blacksmith, village shop and barns, The Pheasant has 16 rooms and its own indoor swimming pool that attracts visitors from across the North of England, Scotland and even regulars from London.

The white table-clothed main dining room, which is open to non-residents, has an elegant ambience, and diners can also eat in the conservatory or outside.

"When the sun is out, we've got a wonderful terrace overlooking the village duck pond and over the fields; everyone loves it," says Peter, who is originally from Leicester. "I've been here for 10 years – I'm a bit of Yorkshireman now. I think they've just about accepted me!"

The Pheasant
POACHED HOTEL HENS EGGS WITH ASPARAGUS, MORELS, POTATA & PEA SHOOTS

One of the most popular dishes on the menu at The Pheasant – we collect the eggs every day from our chickens at the hotel. It's a great combination of flavours and textures, and when served in a ceramic egg, it brings an element of surprise. Serves 4.

Ingredients

4 fresh hen eggs

12 spears asparagus

12 morel mushrooms

20 pea shoots

10g Sosa air bag potata (wheat and potato crunchy topping)

1 lime

250g button mushrooms, sliced

Maldon salt

Milk

White wine vinegar

Xanthan gum

50g butter

1 sprig lemon thyme

100m vegetable oil

Method

Cut the asparagus spears into 10cm pieces and peel from the top down. Blanch in salted boiling water for two minutes and refresh in iced water.

Trim the stalks off the morel mushrooms and wash in cold water. Allow them to dry out on a tea towel. In a frying pan, gently fry the mushrooms in 25g of foaming butter and a sprig of lemon thyme. Drain on a piece of kitchen towel and cool.

In a saucepan, put 25g of butter, the juice and zest of one lime and the sliced button mushrooms. Add a pinch of salt and gently simmer until the mushrooms are fully cooked.

Place the mushrooms and all the liquid into a liquidiser. Add a pinch of xanthan gum and blend until smooth. Season with salt to taste. Add a little milk if it is too thick.

Put 100ml of vegetable oil and the potata into a deep saucepan. Cook on a high heat until the potata puffs up, drain quickly through a sieve and season with salt.

Poach the hen eggs in a tall pan of simmering water with 2.5%-5% of white wine vinegar.

To assemble

Put two tablespoons of the warm mushroom and lime purée in the bottom of a bowl and place the poached egg on top. Cover with the puffed potata crisp.

Warm the morels and asparagus in the oven or under a grill. Then position them through the potata crisp so the asparagus tips face upwards and the morels stand up.

Cut five pea shoots and push them in to the purée so they also stand up and look like they are growing out of the dish. Repeat for the other three servings and serve immediately.

The Pheasant

WILD HALIBUT, LINCOLNSHIRE PRAWN & ARTICHOKE SALAD WITH AVOCADO & SOURDOUGH BREAD

A great visual summer salad with lots of interesting ingredients.
All the preparation is done in advance so it's a great dish to serve for
a dinner party. If you can't find all the ingredients for the salad,
improvise with other items of your choice. Serves 4.

Ingredients

4 x 100g portions wild halibut

8 Lincolnshire king prawns, cooked and peeled

250g sourdough loaf

2 globe artichokes

2 avocadoes

1 lime

Tabasco sauce

2g ascorbic acid

1 red onion

32 roquito peppers

8 sprigs monks beard

Herb sprigs (oregano, burnett, fennel, chive, sorrel)

4 slices pancetta

25ml cabernet sauvignon vinegar

50ml extra virgin rapeseed oil

1 lemon, juiced

4 French breakfast radishes, thinly sliced

1 tsp chopped herbs (chives, parsley, tarragon)

25ml vegetable oil

500ml vegetable stock

Method

Peel the artichokes back to the base and cook in vegetable stock and 1g of the ascorbic acid (or you can use lemon juice) until tender.

Blend the avocado flesh, the juice of the lime and 1g of the ascorbic acid (or a teaspoon of lemon juice) until smooth and season with a couple of drops of Tabasco sauce. Pour into a squeezy bottle or piping bag.

Grill the pancetta slices until they are crispy.

Tear the dough out of the middle of the sourdough loaf so you have 12 mouthful sized pieces. Drizzle a little rapeseed oil on them and fry in a dry pan until they are crispy and golden on the outside.

Cut the red onion into six wedges, separate the petals and cook on a tray in the oven at 140°c until they start to soften.

Thinly slice four French breakfast radishes long-ways and keep in cold water.

Pick and wash the monks beard and other herbs of your choice.

To assemble and serve

Take four large flat plates and place five large dots of the avocado purée in a large circle on each one.

Cut the king prawns in half and place four pieces on each plate. Cut the artichoke hearts into six wedges and place them on each plate, joining up the gaps between the avocado.

Add the red onion petals, sourdough bread croutons, pancetta, roquito peppers and radishes to complete the circular salad on the plate. Garnish the salad with the herb sprigs and monk's beard.

In a hot frying pan, cook the halibut fillets in vegetable oil until golden on one side. Place on a non-stick tray and finish in a low oven at 140°c until cooked.

Drain the excess oil from the pan and return to a low heat. Add the rapeseed oil, vinegar, lemon juice and chopped herbs. As soon as it simmers, pour the mixture in to a jug.

When the halibut is cooked, place in the centre of the salad and serve. Pour the dressing over the whole dish at the table.

STRAWBERRY SHORTCAKE, VANILLA CREAM CHEESE, STRAWBERRY AND ROSE SORBET

This classic pudding is one of our favourites and is hugely popular with the customers. It has a great visual impact at the table as the strawberry consommé is poured over. A perfect early summer dessert. Serves 4.

Ingredients

For the shortcake:

2 egg yolks

80g sugar

200g plain flour

2g salt

100g butter

8g baking powder

For the vanilla cream cheese:

125g clotted cream

225g cream cheese

15g icing sugar

1 vanilla pod

For the strawberry purée:

400g strawberries plus 14 extra equal sized strawberries for serving

40g icing sugar

4g ultratex (available online)

4 tsp lime juice

For the sorbet:

330g strawberry purée

15g rosewater

220g water

110g sugar

1g gellan gum type f

For the consommé:

100g water

50g sugar

50g strawberries

Rose petals made with 1 pink rose and icing sugar

Method

Place all the shortbread ingredients except for the egg yolks into a mixer. Mix on the lowest setting until it looks like golden breadcrumbs. Add the yolks to bind and then chill the mixture in the fridge.

Roll the pastry on a floured surface to 3mm thickness and cut out eight circles with an 85mm fluted cutter. Bake on a non-stick tray at 160°c for 10 minutes.

Beat all the ingredients for the vanilla cream cheese together in a mixer. Put the mixture into a piping bag with a large star shaped nozzle.

For the strawberry purée

Blend the strawberries, icing sugar, lime juice and ultratex in a liquidiser. Pass through a fine sieve and put 100ml in a squeezy bottle, saving the rest for the sorbet.

For the sorbet

Place all the sorbet ingredients into a saucepan and bring to the boil, whisking all the time. Pour into a Pacojet tin and freeze. If you are not using a Pacojet, don't use any gellan gum, instead bring all the ingredients to the boil, chill and churn in an ice cream machine.

For the consommé

Bring the water and sugar to the boil, remove from the heat and add the strawberries. Once cool, pass through a fine sieve.

Pick the petals from the rose, dust with icing sugar and spray with a little water. Dry in a dehydrator or warm cupboard.

To assemble

Place the first shortbread in the middle of a dessert plate. Put the 85mm cutter on it and place six halves of strawberries cut side outwards in a circle around the inside of the cutter.

Fill the centre with the vanilla cream cheese. Remove the cutter and place another shortbread on the top and dust with icing sugar.

Put dots of strawberry purée around the outside. Churn the sorbet in the Pacojet if you are using one. Place one scoop of sorbet on top of the shortbread and garnish with the dried rose petals and half a strawberry. Pour the consommé into a jug and serve at the table.

Country Charm and CHARACTER

Regional produce is central to The Plough Inn at Scalby, which has a great choice of local ales too.

The Plough is part of the HQ Collection – an eclectic mix of destinations to drink, dine and stay in the villages of Scalby and Seamer, near Scarborough. The HQ Collection is owned by Nick and Sandra Thomas, who have lived in Scalby for three decades.

The Plough in Scalby combines a village inn, restaurant and luxurious ensuite accommodation, successfully balancing its role as a local 'pub' and a renowned small luxury hotel.

Local produce is central to The Plough's seasonally changing menus and specials, created by head chef Jon Smith. Jon's focus is on contemporary dishes; perennial favourites include his Scarborough crab salad, avocado, pink grapefruit, garden herbs & crab crisps and Roast Leven duck breast, a little leg meat pie, carrots, turnips, orange and anise. A popular range of 'Yorkshire Tapas' sharing boards are also available along with lighter fare at lunchtimes and, of course, traditional Sunday Roast. Jon comments; "The use of quality fresh produce is the key to our menu. We have built up a network of fantastic local suppliers, including meats from the Stepney Hill Farm, Nockels Butchers, and Edwin Jenkinson for our lobsters and shellfish. I am especially proud of our 'Greenhouse Garden' at The Plough where we grow our own herbs and vegetables. We

also use local cheeses, including the award-winning Yellison goat's cheese, Fountain's Gold cheddar from the Wensleydale Creamery as well as Yorkshire Fine Fettle from Shepherds Purse."

Local isn't confined to food. The Plough serves a wide range of locally-brewed craft ales, and takes its wine selection seriously, working exclusively with renowned Yorkshire-based wine merchants House of Townend. A variety of gins, along with popular cocktails is another Plough specialty – so the guests are never short for choice.

The Plough has been at the heart of Scalby since 1899, but closed in 2011 due to a lack of investment from its national brewery owner and a sequence of failed tenancies. After buying the property in 2013, Nick and Sandra thought carefully about how best to revive its fortunes, resulting in a £1m investment focused on creating a relaxed informal ambience for drinking and dining, complemented by eight comfort cooled ensuite bedrooms on the first and second floors. The Plough also offers a self-contained cottage and an apartment, both with two bedrooms, 'dog friendly' and just a few steps away, adjacent to The Yew Tree Café & Bistro, The Plough's sister establishment in Scalby village.

The Plough Inn

The Plough Inn
SALT BEEF SALAD NIÇOISE WITH CRISPY HEN'S EGG & BLACK OLIVE FLATBREAD

A great combination of flavours and textures combined into a super salad.
Serves 4.

Ingredients

For the salt beef salad:

400g salted beef brisket (a good local butcher should be able to make this for you; get it pre-cooked if you can)

200g fine green beans

400g new potatoes

80g sunblush tomatoes

1 punnet pea shoots

60g marinaded anchovies

80g good quality pitted black olives

Vinaigrette dressing

6 free-range eggs

70g fine white breadcrumbs

100g plain flour

For the black olive flatbread:

10g fresh yeast

90ml tepid water

5g salt

5g sugar

25ml olive oil

210g plain flour

20g pitted black olives, finely chopped

Method

For the flatbread

Dissolve the yeast in the tepid water, then add all the other ingredients into a mixing bowl and pour in the water. Mix into a dough and knead until smooth. Cover the bowl with cling film and leave in a warm place to prove until it has doubled in size.

Remove the dough onto a floured surface and knead again, divide into four equal pieces and roll through a pasta machine on number 2 setting. Lay the sheets out flat and cut into long triangles.

Place on a non-stick baking sheet, brush with oil and sprinkle with sea salt. Bake in the oven at 160°c for 8-10 minutes or until crispy. Keep warm.

For the salad

Gently boil the beef brisket in water for 4 hours and when it's soft, allow it to cool in the water (preferably overnight) to retain its moisture. The next day remove the beef and shred into small pieces.

Cook the new potatoes, cool and slice into small rounds.

Blanch the green beans in rapidly boiling salted water for three minutes, then place in iced water until cold.

Boil four of the eggs for 5½ minutes, then place into iced water until cool. Peel carefully.

Beat the remaining two raw eggs in a bowl. Put the flour and breadcrumbs into two separate bowls.

Very carefully dip the eggs, first into the flour then the beaten eggs, ensuring they are fully coated, and finally into the breadcrumbs.

To assemble

Combine the salt beef, green beans, cooked sliced potatoes, pitted halved olives, sunblush tomatoes, pea shoots and anchovies, and mix gently with the vinaigrette dressing.

Deep fry the breadcrumbed eggs for one minute and leave to rest so the yolk is warm.

Place the salad in four serving bowls. Top each with a crispy egg and a triangle of olive bread. Drizzle with rapeseed oil (we use lemon flavoured at the pub) and serve.

Quarmby's Deli

Quarmby's Delicatessen
EMMA'S CARROT CAKE

Based in Sheriff Hutton, Quarmby's blends together a deli and coffee house where locally-sourced ingredients from specialist producers are sold alongside delicious homemade goodies. Owned by Will and Emma Quarmby, you'll find organic vegetables, pies made by Michael Pern, gorgeous quiches made using seasonal veg from their wonderful in house cook Lynne, real bread from Haxby Bakehouse and superb cakes created by Emma, with plenty of gluten-free and dairy-free choices. Not to mention the extensive range of cheeses on offer. Emma's past as an interior designer is reflected in the coffee house's simple but elegant vibe.

Makes 2 x 23cm round tins or a 23cm x 33cm traybake.

Ingredients

For the cake:

325g gluten-free plain flour (we use Doves or Glebe Farm blends)

225g fairtrade golden caster sugar

1 tsp baking powder (gluten-free)

1 tsp bicarbonate of soda

¾ tsp salt

1 tbsp organic ground cinnamon (we always try to use organic herbs and spices as their flavour is markedly better)

225g dark muscovado sugar

4 large free-range eggs

300ml cold press rapeseed oil (we use Yorkshire rapeseed oil)

450g carrots, grated

For the icing:

300g sieved icing sugar (always sieve – this is one step you cannot skip. I've tried and regretted it every time)

150g full fat cream cheese/ mascarpone (for dairy free use 125g dairy free cream cheese such as Tofutti)

50g butter (for dairy free, use dairy free margarine)

Method

For the cake

Beat the eggs and dark brown muscovado sugar until the sugar has dissolved, using a balloon whisk or in a mixer with a K blade fitted. Add the oil and beat again to combine.

In a separate bowl, gather all the remaining dry ingredients and give them a brief whisk to evenly distribute.

Add the wet to the dry ingredients and fold together until well combined and no traces of flour remain. Fold in the grated carrots.

Preheat the oven to 190°c or 180°c for a fan oven.

Divide the mixture between your two tins or into the single traybake tin with the sides oiled and lined with baking parchment.

Bake for 40-45 minutes until risen and firm. Use your finger to test resistance, there should be a springiness to the centre of your cakes – the surface may be slightly bubbly looking but this is normal.

Stand in the tin for 10 minutes before removing and cooling on cooling racks. Leave to cool completely before icing.

For the icing

Put all the ingredients into a food processor (I always go for the easy option as life is short – although this can be done with an electric hand whisk or with elbow grease and a wooden spoon).

Whizz until just combined, too long and it will break down the icing too much and it will become very runny. If this happens don't worry, simply add some more sieved icing sugar and stir through until perfectly smooth. If you're making this whilst the cakes cook set aside in the fridge until you're ready to use.

Take the icing out of the fridge 10-15 minutes before you need it to allow it to loosen up. If it's still a bit firm just work it with your palette knife until it becomes pliable.

Divide the icing in half and cover the first cake generously then sandwich the other cake on top and give it a final flourish of ground cinnamon if you like.

Variation

If you enjoy a nutty crunch, add 50g of slightly crushed walnuts (use your fist) at the same time as the carrots.

Fish, Chips, Cocktails...
AND VAMPIRES

Sustainable fish from Whitby's national award winner Quayside is the perfect dish for a day on the North Yorkshire coast.

A trip to the seaside isn't complete without fish and chips, but not every chippie has a cocktail bar above it … or a historic connection to Dracula author, Bram Stoker.

Quayside on the harbour at Whitby can boast both – plus some of the finest fish and chips you'll sample anywhere.

"The Quayside building had a bath house on the first floor for fishermen and the second floor was the town library," says Stuart Fusco, whose family have been frying fish and chips in Whitby for three generations.

"It's well documented that Bram Stoker did a lot of his research and notes before he wrote Dracula from the Quayside second floor; from there you can see right over to Tate Hill Beach."

Today, the second floor is home to Bar 7, a cocktail bar that's run by the family, who came over from Naples in the 1890's. But for the real foodie action, you need to go downstairs to the fish and chip takeaway and restaurant that was crowned National Fish and Chip Shop of the Year in 2014.

Stuart says: "We have been serving fish and chips in Whitby since 1968 and it all started with my grandmother, Violet, in Pickering in the 1950s.

"We were the first fish and chip shop in Yorkshire to achieve the Marine Stewardship Council certificate for sustainability. All the cod and haddock is traceable back to the boat it was caught on and has been correctly managed through the supply chain. Also, all of our potatoes come from Yorkshire."

Having sustainable fish on the menu is tremendously important to us; we are a longstanding family business and have had the pleasure of serving local families for many years now. We want this to continue and this means we need to be certain of the fish stocks for years to come. For us, the way to do that is to purchase sustainable fish and the MSC is the voice of sustainability," he added.

Diners in the restaurant have a good choice of meals, with different seafood dishes, children's meals and gluten-free options available.

"Fish and chips is one of those wonderful dishes that is synonymous with a day at the seaside and Whitby is known for its fish and chips, as it has more fish and chip shops per square mile than anywhere else.

"I think everyone has a soft spot for fish and chips."

Quayside Fish and Chips
FUSCO'S FISH PIE

A different combination of Quayside's key ingredients of fish and potatoes. This classic fish pie, which includes eggs for added flavour and texture, is among the alternative dishes you'll find at the top Whitby fish and chip restaurant. Serves 6.

Ingredients

1kg Maris Piper potatoes

900g fish (a mixture of mostly white fish such as cod, haddock and pollock works best. Salmon and prawns are a good addition for colour, texture and extra flavour)

850ml milk

50g butter

50g plain flour

Handful fresh parsley, chopped

1 carrot, grated

2 eggs

Handful of cheddar cheese, grated

Method

Preheat the oven to 200°c.

Peel the potatoes, place in a saucepan and cover with water. Bring to the boil and simmer until tender. Once cooked, drain thoroughly and mash, adding a splash of milk and a knob of butter. Season to taste.

Place the two eggs in a pan, cover with water and bring to the boil. Boil for 7 minutes, remove from the heat and drain. Set the eggs aside.

Meanwhile, pour the milk into a non-stick pan on a medium to low heat, allowing the milk to heat up slowly so it is fairly hot but not boiling. Add the fish and cook for 10-15 minutes, keeping a close eye so that the milk doesn't boil. Don't agitate the fish too much as it will break up.

Once cooked, carefully scoop out the fish with a slotted spoon and place it in an ovenproof dish. Set aside the milk as it is required for the sauce. Peel the cooked eggs and cut into quarters and place in the dish with the fish.

Melt the butter in a pan, stir in the flour and cook the mixture for just under a minute. Gradually whisk in the milk leftover from cooking the fish. Bring to the boil, stirring to avoid any lumps and to stop the sauce sticking to the bottom of the pan. Cook for 3-4 minutes until thickened. (You may not need all of the milk, it depends how much liquor comes out of the fish during cooking). Season to taste.

Stir in the chopped parsley and grated carrot. Pour the sauce over the fish and eggs.

Spoon on the mashed potatoes and sprinkle the cheese over evenly. Bake for around 10-20 minutes, until the cheese is melted and golden brown.

Serve with fresh green vegetables.

Nice and SPICY

Quality spices and curry mixes, hand-blended to original family recipes, are the hallmark of York-based Rafi's Spicebox.

Rafi's Spicebox is all about adding some authentic zing to home cooked Indian food, making cooking with spices accessible and giving people the confidence to cook amazing food at home.

Founded by the late Rafi Fernandez in 1989, the spice mixes are still blended by hand using her recipes. Rafi, who wrote 10 cookery books, came to UK in 1965 and originally set up the business in Suffolk. Today, it's still a small, family business, headed by her sons Kevin and Lee and a passionate team of foodies.

Kevin said: "After mum wrote her first book she discovered there might be an opportunity to introduce spices and Asian ingredients to small rural areas that had not seen them before.

She would give them teaspoons of various spices and handwrite instructions for them. It was a way of putting great quality spices into people's hands and inspiring them to cook Indian food. That concept has developed since then, and the 'curry pack' is now what we're known for!"

The spices, which are also available loose, are mainly imported from India. The knowledgeable Spicebox team then hand-mix the spices, fresh to order, to produce a variety of 'curry packs', with simple to use recipes. An important part of this tailored service is the personal touch provided by the team, who are always enthusiastic to share their tips, provide suggestions for recipes that use in-season produce and give advice for planning menus. There are also lots of these tips and recipe ideas available on the Spicebox website.

Originally six spice mixes were available, but with constant development Rafi's Spicebox now produce more than forty different mixes including seasonal specials, family recipes and interpretations of classic, regional dishes.

You'll also find a variety of gift sets, pickles and chutneys from traditional Indian brands and UK artisan producers, plus rice, breads, snacks, kitchenware items and other interesting world food products.

Whether you are a novice cook or a kitchen guru, the friendly Spicebox team are always eager to share their experiences and knowledge to help you get the most out of your spices.

Rali's Spicebox
MOGHUL-STYLE ROAST LAMB (SHAHI RAAN)

Perfect for a relaxed weekend meal with the family. In India this is a celebration dish often enjoyed at weddings. It's a real show stopper - whilst still being easy - so it's great for a dinner party. The spice mixture is very versatile and you could use it on lamb chops, a beef joint or a chicken, and if there are any leftovers, it makes incredible chicken sarnies. Serves 4-6.

Ingredients

4 onions, chopped

4 cloves garlic

5cm piece of fresh ginger

3 tbsp ground almonds

2 tsp cumin powder

2 tsp coriander powder

2 tsp turmeric

2 tsp garam masala

4-6 green chillies

Juice of one lemon

Salt, to taste

300ml natural yoghurt

1tsp black cumin

Leg of lamb (about 1.8kg in weight)

Toasted flaked almonds, to garnish

Method

In a food processor blend the first 11 ingredients to make a smooth paste. Gradually add the yoghurt, mixing well, then stir through the black cumin.

Make four or five incisions into the lamb. Place it on a baking tray and rub the spice mixture into the cuts and all over the surface of the lamb.

Cover the tray loosely with foil and roast for 2-2½ hours at 190°c. Remove the foil for the last 10 minutes of cooking.

Allow the meat to rest for 10-15 minutes before carving. Garnish with toasted flaked almonds.

We like to serve this dish simply, with tomatoes roasted with chilli flakes and salt, a lentil dish (dhal), fried greens with garlic and ajwain seeds, and chapatis.

Robinsons Café
CHORIZO, PARMA HAM AND SUNDRIED TOMATO HASH

Tasty food made from locally sourced ingredients supplied by independent traders is the ethos of family-run Robinsons on York's Bishopthorpe Road. Opened in 2016 by Will Pearce and Rebecca Toppin – and named in honour of Will's mum's maiden name and his middle name – Robinsons offers breakfast, brunch and lunch options throughout the day, as well as regularly changing specials and treats, plus quality coffee and alcoholic drinks.

Serves 2.

Ingredients

500g new potatoes

400g chorizo

6 slices Parma ham

200g sundried tomatoes

200g spinach

4 free-range eggs

Balsamic glaze

Salt and pepper

Olive oil

2 tsp white wine vinegar (for poaching eggs)

Method

Cook the potatoes in a pan of salted water until soft. Drain and leave to cool slightly. Once the potatoes are cool enough to handle cut into quarters.

Take the outer skin off the chorizo and dice into 2cm cubes. Slice the Parma ham the same way as the chorizo.

Heat a frying pan over a high heat. Add a splash of olive oil and add the potatoes. Fry until golden.

Add the cubed chorizo and fry for 2 minutes. Add the chopped Parma ham and continue to fry for a further 2 minutes.

Fill a saucepan three-quarters full with water and add the vinegar. This will be used for poaching the eggs. Bring the water to a simmer and crack in the eggs one at a time. Poach for 2-3 minutes and when they are cooked, remove from the water and leave to drain on a kitchen cloth.

Once the chorizo, potatoes and Parma ham are nicely coloured, add the sundried tomatoes and spinach. Lower the heat and lightly toss all the ingredients together until the spinach has wilted. Season with salt and pepper and divide between two bowls.

Place the cooked poached eggs on top of the hash and drizzle the balsamic glaze over the top.

A Most Unusual
TEA ROOM

Step inside Whitby's Rusty Shears Tea Room for a blend of vintage and contemporary, and a huge selection of gins alongside hot drinks and tasty food.

If quirky cafés are your thing, it's worth your while seeking out Rusty Shears 'most unusual' tea room, with its own courtyard compete with brollies, heaters and blankets hiding behind an iron gate.

Inside the café itself, you'll discover a venue that muddles up the modern and retro, and has more than 100 gins available alongside the traditional and imaginative fare that's on offer.

Owners Kirstie Shears and Russell Hirst combined their names to create Rusty Shears when they took over the café in 2014, and they have really put their own stamp on things. Kirstie swapped her career in clothing at Marks & Spencer head office for cooking; conversely, Russell, who was a baker, is now front of house.

Kirstie said: "Everything is baked here fresh in the morning; the only thing I buy in is pork pies from the local butcher.

"We do sharing boards – meat, cheese and vegetarian ones. I'm a vegetarian so we have lots of vegetarian choices."

The Rusty Shears menu includes plenty of unusual dishes to complement the quirky décor, from mushroom burgers to Moroccan lamb, a fabulous choice of cakes and teas and a range of gluten-free and vegan options. As much local produce is used as possible, both from the nearby greengrocer and from customers who bring in home-grown goodies.

"Our regulars with allotments bring us loads of food," said Kirstie.

"From rhubarb to leeks, we try to use everything they give us, and we pay them in cakes and coffees."

The café was a licensed premises when Kirstie and Russell took over, and they've developed the alcohol side with a large choice of unusual gins.

Kirstie said: "We both like gin and we got more in. It escalated from there, and from 5pm-8pm during peak season, we have gin evenings with cocktails."

Visitors will also find regular live music at the venue, a gift shop that proudly stocks Annie Sloan chalk paints, and a place where their dog is welcome to join them both inside the café as well as the courtyard.

Rusty Shears Tea Room
BEETROOT AND FETA BURGERS WITH MINT YOGHURT AND HERB SALAD

Ingredients

For the burgers:

300g beetroot, cooked, peeled and coarsely grated

200g feta cheese, crumbled

3 tbsp mint, chopped

3 tbsp dill, chopped

4 shallots, finely sliced

2 spring onions, finely sliced

3 eggs, beaten

200g fresh breadcrumbs

100g plain flour

2 tbsp olive oil

For the yoghurt:

200g Greek yoghurt

2 tbsp mint, chopped

Squeeze of lemon juice

For the herb salad:

2 tbsp dill

2 tbsp mint

3 shallots, finely sliced

Sliced cucumber

Baby leaf salad

4 ciabatta buns

Method

Drain the grated beetroot and pat dry with kitchen roll. Tip into a bowl and stir in the feta, spring onions, herbs, eggs, flour and breadcrumbs. Season and shape into 4 burgers.

Heat the olive oil in a large frying pan, add the burgers and cook for 4-5 minutes each side until firm and golden. Meanwhile, mix the yoghurt with the mint and lemon juice and toast the ciabatta buns in the oven.

Mix the ingredients for the herb salad together.

To assemble

Spread the mint yoghurt on both sides of the bun, then add the herb salad and layer the sliced cucumber on top.

Top the salad with the burger and add a squeeze of lemon before adding baby leaf salad and the bun lid.

Simply STEAK

Top quality beef and a friendly family ambience mean The Rythre Arms is probably the best-known steakhouse in Yorkshire.

"I'm a glorified shopper", says The Rythre Arms' owner Tony Linley of his never-ending quest to ensure the specialist steak venue always has the very best meat.

"I'm out at least three days a week purchasing and I do a couple of days' homework, going down to the market to find out what's going through. I'll buy from whoever has the best beef at the time."

Although a good proportion of the steak that does pass through The Rythre Arms' kitchen is North Yorkshire-produced, Tony won't reduce the quality for the sake of buying local.

He said: "All our reputation is built about the quality of the beef. But in North Yorkshire, we've got a lot of smaller producers that really do care about their produce.

"A lot of farmers are producing really good beef stock and taking pride in the way they rear the animals. When I go to farmers' markets and they're proud of the product they're taking, they are the ones I want to buy from."

Tony and wife Lisa have been at the helm at The Rythre Arms since 1997, when they took over from his father, who was a slaughterman before becoming a restaurateur. Tony's spent his life cheffing, and the restaurant is a real family affair with his mother-in-law and brother-in-law also on the staff.

Originally a centuries-old pub, the Linleys converted The Rythre Arms into a comfortable and cosy steak venue, where Tony says "we do glorify the cow". You'll find subtle cow-hide wallpaper and artworks paying homage to the source of the steaks, which range in size from 6oz to the giant 78oz Rythre Monster.

The food and the ambience goes down well with staff and customers. Most of the employees have at least 10 years' service under their belts, and the restaurant has a loyal customer base, many of whom have been celebrating key milestones there for years.

"We get to know people really well," says Tony.

"We have 21-year-olds coming for their birthdays and their parents came for their 21st too. We are an occasion place, but it's warm and family-led."

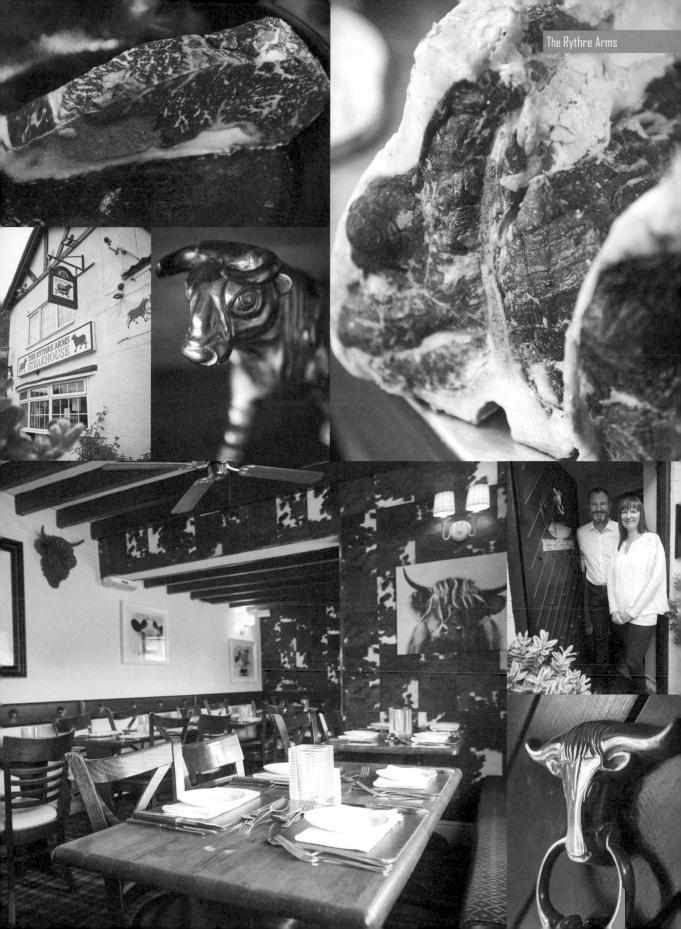

The Rythre Arms
THE RYTHRE PEPPER SAUCE

Plus a guide to buying and cooking great steak at home. Serves up to 6.

Ingredients

1 shallot, finely chopped

30g butter

1 level tbsp brined green peppercorns

1 heaped tsp cracked black pepper

1 level tsp ground white pepper (less if you prefer it milder)

3 tbsp cognac

420ml double cream

420ml demi-glace or a decent homemade beef gravy

Method

Warm the butter in a medium saucepan and add the finely chopped shallot. Cook gently until they have softened and are slightly translucent.

Add the green peppercorns and both dry peppers. Cook on a low heat for a couple of minutes, stirring with a wooden spoon.

Remove from the heat and add the cognac, demi-glace or gravy and cream. Be careful near naked flames when placing it back on the heat.

Bring the pan to a slow simmer and reduce to the desired consistency, stirring all the time. Taste and add salt if required.

How to choose the best steak

The best way is to use a good independent butcher but if you have to buy from the supermarket, here are some tips.

Good beef needs to be aged for flavour and tenderness, so ideally look for 28 day dry aged.

Do not be put off by a steak that's dark red or nearly brown; if the packaging is intact and the best before date hasn't been exceeded (too much) it's just the natural colouration of matured beef.

The next and most important thing to look for is fat, not just the important heavy marbling in rib-eyes, but also the line around the outside of a sirloin or a rump. Don't think you are paying good money for something you won't be eating; if it doesn't have fat on the outside, the meat will not eat well. Generally, the fattier the steak the better it will be.

Once you've found that perfect steak, you need to get it out of its packaging the day before you intend to cook. Place on a plate on the bottom shelf of the fridge with another plate on top to cover – don't use cling film, you need the meat to breathe.

2 hours before you intend to cook, remove from the fridge and allow it to reach room temperature.

You should always cook steak on a high heat initially to seal the outside, then turn it down to finish cooking. Ideally in a heavy, flat bottomed frying pan, never under the grill.

If you are cooking sirloin or rump, try to stand the steak on the fat edge to start rendering the fat first. This will also remove the need for any extra oil. You can season if desired but keep it simple with just some quality sea salt.

Cook to your liking but remember that rib-eyes should be cooked medium rare or over to allow the fat chance to cook too.

Skosh
SMOKED COD'S ROE CREAM, SALMON 'CAVIAR' & POTATO CRISPS

Asian-influenced food on small plates is the essence of Skosh – which is abbreviated Japanese slang for 'a little bit'. Chef Neil Bentinck opened the business in York mid-2016 to offer a modern approach to a grazing menu, where diners can choose a multitude of eclectic snacks, savoury and sweet plates for their meal. Whether you have them all served at once or one after the other is your choice. "It's a hybrid of the tasting menu and a chef's view of Asian street food," says Neil. "It's refined on the plate and served in a relaxed, cool, urban atmosphere."

Serves 8 as part of a grazing menu or nibbles with drinks.

Ingredients

For the cod's roe cream:

200g smoked cod's roe

50ml hot water

½ garlic clove, minced

200g extra virgin olive oil

200g vegetable oil

Lemon juice

Table salt

For the salmon 'caviar':

1 small jar of salmon keta 'caviar'

1 tbsp mirin

1 tsp light soy

To finish:

Good quality salted crisps

Chopped chives

Togarashi spice

Method

For the cod's roe cream

Peel the skin from the cod's roe with a small knife and place the flesh in a blender with the hot water.

Blend to a paste with the garlic for one minute. Slowly drizzle in the oils whilst blending to emulsify as if you were making a mayonnaise. Season to taste with the lemon juice and salt.

If it's very thick, slowly add a few tablespoons of hot water to loosen slightly. Place in a piping bag and leave in the fridge until required.

For the salmon 'caviar'

Tip the keta into a small bowl and rinse with cold water. This removes any impurities and produces a brighter colour. Drain well and add the mirin and soy. Set aside.

To serve

Pipe the cod's roe cream into a small serving bowl, top with some of the salmon 'caviar' and sprinkle with chives and Togarashi spice. Serve with the crisps and maybe a glass of bubbly.

Spirit of HARROGATE

With more than half of its specially selected botanicals sourced from the spa town, Slingsby Gin is a real tonic if you love a local tipple.

Named after William Slingsby, the man who discovered the unique properties of the natural spring water from the Tewit Well and turned Harrogate into the Yorkshire spa town it is today, Slingsby Gin is set to put the town on the map again – this time among gin connoisseurs.

And there are plenty of them; there's been a huge revival of interest in the juniper-flavoured spirit in recent years due to the cocktail culture and a new generation of drinkers discovering the refreshing properties of a good G&T.

Slingsby Gin is a 42 percent ABV citrus-based gin that's packed with flavours that distil 'the Spirit of Harrogate' into an eye-catching apothecary style blue glass bottle.

Marcus Black, Slingsby Gin co-founder and joint managing director, said: "We wanted to create a gin that epitomises Harrogate and its spa town heritage. For many years people have visited our beautiful Yorkshire town to restore mind, body and soul by relaxing, indulging and socialising.

"The key ingredients in our gin are hand-grown local botanicals that are synonymous with the beautiful and restorative nature of Harrogate. Some come from the Rudding Park Hotel's kitchen garden and there's green and jasmine tea from Taylor's of Harrogate in there. These are all brought together with water drawn from the world famous Harrogate aquifer."

Only created in 2015, Slingsby Gin is available in more than 200 bars and restaurants and has already picked up prestigious awards – silver medal at San Francisco World Spirits competition and three gold medals at the Spirits Business – Gin Masters for its London Dry and Rhubarb Gin.

Mike Carthy, fellow co-founder and joint managing director, said: "It's truly brilliant and a testament to our hard-working team to be recognised amongst leading brands on a global scale."

Closer to home, visitors to the Spirit of Harrogate shop can book onto different gin tasting experiences. They include a range of activities from tastings to mixology classes, and with more than 90 gins and 60 different types of tonic waters available, there's plenty to choose from. There's even an opportunity to try the special development gins being created in the old fashioned apothecary-style shop. This is where Slingsby's award-winning rhubarb gin first started; it proved so popular the team decided to launch it as a commercially-available product.

"Gin has always been popular, but people are becoming more mindful about the provenance of the drinks they choose," says Mike.

"Slingsby Gin really delves down to where the ingredients have come from."

Slingsby Gin
PARKIN COCKTAIL

Gin is certainly having a moment. Slingsby Gin is great in a classic gin and tonic but it also lends itself beautifully to a range of cocktails. Here are two favourites to tempt your taste buds concocted by Slingsby's master mixologist. Both serve 1.

Ingredients

For the cocktail:

35ml Slingsby Gin

15ml King's ginger liqueur

20ml fresh lime juice

35ml ginger and treacle syrup

Soda

Fresh ginger for garnish

Lime for garish

For the ginger and treacle syrup:

120g fresh ginger, peeled and thinly sliced (start with 200g ginger root)

400g caster sugar

4 tbsp treacle

2 tbsp honey

500ml water

1 tsp all spice

1 tsp black peppercorns

3 star anise

Method

For the ginger and treacle syrup

Combine all the ingredients in a saucepan and simmer on a low heat for about 15 minutes until a syrup-like consistency is reached. Leave to cool, then strain into a clean bottle.

For the cocktail

Shake the cocktail ingredients together and strain into a tall glass with ice. Top up with soda and garnish with a lime twist and fresh ginger.

Slingsby Gin
RASPBERRY AND RHUBARB BRAMBLE

Ingredients

For the cocktail:

35ml rhubarb gin

15ml raspberry liqueur (Chambord)

25ml fresh lemon juice

25ml sweet rhubarb tea syrup

Raspberries for garnish

For the rhubarb tea syrup:

250ml boiling water

250g caster sugar

8 Taylors sweet rhubarb tea bags

Method

For the rhubarb tea syrup

Stir the sugar into the boiling water until it is completely dissolved. Add the teabags and leave them in to brew until the syrup is cold.

For the cocktail

Shake the cocktail ingredients together and strain into a tall glass with ice. Garnish with three raspberries.

Baby you're a STAR

Dining at the 14th century thatched Star Inn at Harome is like stepping into another world.

"It's a bit like The Good Life," says Andrew Pern, as he describes the foraging chickens, rare breed pigs and beehives that visitors encounter when they arrive at The Star Inn at Harome.

Dating back to the 1300s and boasting a coffee loft and private dining area under the thatched eaves that used to be a dormitory for travelling monks, the Inn has been Michelin-starred for 12 years.

Local lad Andrew, a farmer's son who was born in Whitby and lived in the Esk Valley, has been at the helm for two decades and is the creator of a menu that Michelin describes as 'modern Yorkshire' in style.

"I was brought up with good food and the seasons," he says.

"We use that as the starting point and let the seasons write our menus. That's it – with a bit of fine tuning."

As well as the home-reared pork, fresh eggs and honey, the inn also uses ingredients from its large kitchen garden, where the team has planted 60 different fruit and nut trees. At one point, Andrew also had his own herd of 22 Highland cattle too.

The proximity of the coast means there's a strong seafood element to the menu, with Whitby crab and lobster, turbot and halibut arriving fresh in the kitchens every day.

"We've used the same suppliers for more than 25 years," said Andrew.

"We have a good relationship with them and they've become friends."

The Star Inn also has a long association with Andrew's own family. His parents and grandparents used to visit in their youth, and Andrew also has fond memories of the inn when he was growing up.

Inside the thatched building, which has had a dwelling on site since the 9th century, is a bar decked out with Mousey Thompson furniture. The Star Inn was the first that the famous Yorkshire craftsman furnished back in 1931. Variations on the mouse theme are found throughout the inn, which has a nine bedroom-lodge for overnight stays.

Andrew said: "When people come here from towns and cities they come into our own little world – a quintessential English village with a duck pond, a church and a thatched inn.

"We're very much a chapter in the history of the Star Inn; we look after it and nurture it. We have five children, and hopefully one of them will take it on."

POCKLEY 3

The Star Inn at Harome

GRILLED BLACK PUDDING WITH PAN-FRIED FOIE GRAS, PICKERING WATERCRESS, APPLE & VANILLA CHUTNEY AND SCRUMPY REDUCTION

A tasty treat mixing Yorkshire and continental ingredients with flavoursome homemade chutney. Serves 1 though easily scalable.

Ingredients

10g watercress, washed and trimmed

Salt and pepper

Knob of butter

Sprigs of thyme, for garnish

2 slices black pudding

1 slice caramelised apple

1 decent slice of duck or goose foie gras

Apple juice

A splash of cider vinegar

A dash of vinaigrette

For the apple and vanilla chutney:

1kg Granny Smith apples with skin, diced into ½–1cm pieces

3 medium shallots, finely diced

200ml cider vinegar (or white wine, if you wish)

1 fresh vanilla pod, split and deseeded

400g caster sugar

Pinch of salt

Method

For the apple & vanilla chutney

Place everything into an ample-sized thick-bottomed pan and reduce down until thickened and starting to caramelise. Cool down and tub up ready for using. Keep in a cool place.

N.B. Place the vanilla pod into the pan with everything else to maximise the flavour.

To serve

Make the scrumpy reduction by reducing the apple juice and cider vinegar together.

Place five small piles of apple chutney at intervals around the plate and garnish each pile with a sprig of thyme.

In the centre of the plate, dress a few seasoned leaves of watercress to form a little salad. Drizzle the scrumpy reduction around the side of the plate.

Lightly brush the slices of black pudding with melted butter and grill for 3-4 minutes. Whilst this is cooking, heat a frying pan and fry the foie gras for 1½ minutes on each side.

When cooked, stack alternatively black pudding, foie gras, black pudding. Top with the slice of caramelised apple. Serve immediately.

Deli and JELLY

The Whitby Deli combines local and continental goodies, including the fresh taste of Yorkshire-made Just Jelly.

Although it opened at Hallowe'en 2014, coinciding with the town's famous twice-yearly Goth Weekend, The Whitby Deli's certainly not a scary place to visit.

"There's a pre-conception that delis are expensive and exclusive, and we're really not," says owner Catherine Cook.

"We want people to come in; we offer quality produce and are better value than supermarkets for our cured meats."

Inside you'll discover a mixture of Yorkshire and continental treats, from cooked meats and antipasti to local cheeses, craft beers, organic wines, coffee and a wide range of larder essentials, alternatively you can take a seat and enjoy one of the many home cooked dishes in the delis vibrant dining area.

Catherine said "We showcase lots of local cheeses and award-winning varieties from smaller artisan producers."

Catherine, who is originally from Teesside, moved back north with her husband after managing a barristers' chambers in London to follow what she calls her "pipe dream" of opening a deli. Deliberately choosing the non-touristy part of town as a location, she's building The Whitby Deli into a foodie business for local people.

"We do our own brand of Whitby Deli wine, our own brand biscuits and our own range of preserves, pickles and chutneys.

"We champion Yorkshire products and ingredients and work alongside Ryan from Just Jelly, selling his products and using them in the dishes we produce."

Ryan Tindall started Just Jelly in 2014, using recipes he adapted from his grandmother Elizabeth's recipes. The range includes different jellies infused with mint, Port, beetroot and rosemary, which can transform meat and fish dishes into something a bit special.

Ryan said: "The ideas came from my Yorkshire gran. She used to make mint jelly when I was a kid and one day, I tried making it myself.

"We sell it in delis, farm shops, farmers' markets and online, and we've been taking it to speciality food shows."

The Yorkshire taste of Just Jelly has proved a hit with the Artisan Food Club in London and Ryan is eventually aiming to stock it in supermarkets and high-end retailers.

But if you want a taste of what it can do for a meal, it's worth checking out The Whitby Deli's menu – or trying the recipe overleaf.

Whitby Deli & Just Jelly

LEMON AND ROSEMARY
CHICKEN RISOTTO

Lemony butterflied chicken breasts served with risotto and flavoured with the unique taste of Rosemary Just Jelly. Perfect companions in this quick and easy supper dish. Serves 4.

Ingredients

600ml chicken stock

25g salted butter

1 tbsp olive oil

1 white onion, finely chopped

2 cloves garlic, finely chopped

175ml dry white wine

200g risotto rice

Sea salt

Pepper

1 lemon, zested and juiced

1 tbsp Rosemary Just Jelly

4 free-range chicken breasts, butterflied

Method

Heat the chicken stock in a saucepan.

In a separate pan, melt the butter and fry the finely chopped onion and garlic until soft.

Add the risotto rice and cook for 2-3 minutes.

Turn up the heat and add the wine, once the wine is cooked out turn down the heat to low.

Gradually add the warmed stock, leaving time for the rice to absorb it all slowly. Leave to cook for around 15 minutes.

After the rice is cooked, remove from the heat and stir in the Rosemary Just Jelly and season with salt and pepper.

Leave the risotto to stand and heat the olive oil in a frying pan ready to cook the chicken.

Pan-fry the chicken for 3 minutes on each side with the lemon juice and zest.

Once the chicken is cooked, serve with the rosemary risotto.

A Dales DELIGHT

Based in the beautiful Yorkshire Dales, The White Hart Country Inn in Hawes is earning itself a place on the must-visit map for its culinary credentials.

Yorkshire food, sourced from as close as possible to create quality dishes from scratch, is central to the foodie ethos at The White Hart Country Inn.

Set in the cobbled Main Street in tourist honeypot Hawes, the 18th century coaching inn brings together the traditional and modern, and the same could be said about the cooking style. The kitchen uses tried and tested methods to make its own stock on site from bones and whips up its own ice cream on the premises. Meat comes from a local butcher who rears his own animals and cheese from nearby producers.

"Our head chef, Luke, is passionate about food and especially Yorkshire food," says Helen Wood who has recently taken over running the inn.

"We are a pub, but that's no reason why we can't go all out to give people a good experience and food that's as local as it possibly can be."

The Kirkbride family bought the pub 5 years ago and have gradually developed it into a food destination.

"We are continuing that with a focus on very local Yorkshire produce. We've got a real star in our head chef and he's keen to work with us to create dishes that showcase the produce of Yorkshire."

Diners can eat in the bar during the day and the restaurant at night, choosing from a menu that makes the most of very local, seasonal produce in quality dishes. Due to its fantastic location, the inn attracts a mix of tourists and locals, especially in the evening.

At 850ft above sea-level, Hawes may be on the tourist map as the highest market town in England. But it looks like The White Hart Country Inn is set to turn the town into a must-visit gastronomic location too.

White Hart Country Inn

CRISPY PORK BELLY, BLACK PUDDING CROQUETTES WITH APPLE JELLY AND SMOKED CHEESE

This dish is all about preparation. It is best made the day before, allowing you time to prepare other courses and be ready to wow your guests and still enjoy the party. Serves 6.

Ingredients

For the pork belly:

½ rare breed pork belly (supplied by Nigel Hammond of Hammonds Butchers, Bainbridge)

1 litre good quality local cider, such as Ampleforth Abbey Cider

Spice bag of 1 tsp fennel seeds, 2 star anise and 1 tsp pink peppercorns tied together

Black pudding croquettes:

100g good quality black pudding (we use Cockett's)

200g potatoes, mashed dry

½ leek, finely diced

1 banana shallot, finely diced

20g wholegrain mustard

5 fresh sage leaves, finely chopped

200g homemade white breadcrumbs

200g plain flour

2 medium eggs

100ml milk

For the apple jelly:

300ml Duskins or similar Bramley apple juice

3g agar agar

For the sauce:

4 litres homemade chicken stock and cooking liquor from belly pork, fat skimmed off

1 litre sharp dry cider

5 Bramley apples

The ribs removed from the pork belly - chopped

Small bunch of fresh thyme

½ bulb garlic

100ml double cream

Smoked cheese to dress – we use Smoked Richmond Cheese

2 onions, chopped

Method

For the belly pork

Heat the oven to 150°c, place the belly pork and all other ingredients into an oven proof dish, cover with greaseproof paper and then foil. Braise in the oven for 5 hours. Remove from the oven, taking care not to disturb the tender piece of pork.

Strain the liquor and set aside to use in the sauce.

Press the belly pork in the fridge between two chopping boards, weighed down (we use a roasting tin filled with water).

The next day, when cold and set, trim the edges and cut into 6 equal sized pieces.

For the black pudding and leek croquette

Sweat off the leeks and shallot in oil until soft on a medium heat, but don't colour. Add the other ingredients, season and mix thoroughly. Put into a piping bag.

Place three layers of cling film on your chopping board and pipe out in a line. Roll up and tie the ends securely. Freeze overnight, then portion into 6 cylinders.

Coat each in egg, flour then breadcrumbs.

For the apple jelly

Boil the apple juice, add the agar agar and cook for 2 minutes. Pour into a lightly oiled container and refrigerate. When set, tap out from the container and dice into squares.

Place these back in the tub and set aside.

For the sauce

Heat a heavy-bottomed saucepan until raging hot. Add the rib bones, garlic, thyme, apples and onions then caramelise, scraping off the bottom to stop them from sticking. Add the cider to deglaze and reduce by two-thirds. Add the remaining wet ingredients except the cream and reduce into a thick sauce. Pass through a sieve and add the cream.

To serve

Heat the oven to 180°c.

Pan fry the belly pork pieces skin side down until crispy and well coloured, colour the remaining sides and transfer to the oven for 15 minutes.

After 7 minutes, deep fry the croquettes (180°c if you have a deep fat fryer) until golden.

Serve each pork piece at an angle and trim one end of each croquette flat and stand on end next to the belly pork. Crumble the cheese and scatter 4-6 pieces of the cheese and 4-5 dices of the apple jelly around the plate.

Serve with fresh seasonal vegetables.

White Hart Country Inn
A TASTE OF YORKSHIRE RHUBARB

A show-stopper of a pudding, with homemade ice cream and brûlée that needs
to be started the day before you plan to eat it.
Serves 6.

Ingredients

For the crumble:

320g plain flour

160g cold butter, diced

180g soft brown sugar

100g porridge oats

½ tsp ground ginger

For the quick brûlée:

550ml double cream

4 medium eggs

2 vanilla pods

100g caster sugar plus 50g extra for
the glazed topping

For the rhubarb compote:

1kg fresh rhubarb, chopped

1½ oranges, zested and juiced

2 pieces stem ginger, finely grated

350g caster sugar

For the ice cream:

250g of the rhubarb compote, blended
until very smooth

150ml whole milk

250ml double cream

150g trimoline (inverted sugar –
substitute glucose if necessary)

75g caster sugar

2 drops red food colouring

For the vanilla custard:

300ml whole milk

300ml double cream

8 egg yolks

75g caster sugar

2 vanilla pods, seeds scraped out

Method

For the compote

Place the chopped rhubarb and all remaining ingredients into a heavy bottomed pan. Cook on a medium heat until soft. Reduce in volume for around 10 minutes.

Put a tablespoon of compote into six espresso cups and set aside the rest for the crumble and ice cream.

For the ice cream

Add 250g of smooth rhubarb compote to a heavy bottom pan on a medium heat. Reduce in volume by half to remove the water and prevent ice crystals forming in the ice cream.

Add the remaining ingredients and heat until only just on the boil. Add the food colouring and remove from the heat. Chill and then churn in an ice-cream maker. Freeze until required.

For the crumble

Rub the flour and butter together until the mix resembles breadcrumbs. Add the remaining ingredients, line a baking tray with parchment and bake at 160°c for 12-15 minutes until golden brown.

Stir thoroughly several times during baking to prevent clumping and achieve an even bake. Set aside to cool.

For the quick brûlée

Whisk together the sugar and eggs in a bowl until light and fluffy. Heat the cream with the split vanilla pod then whisk into the sugar and egg mixture. Return to the heat and cook until the mix reaches 87°c or coats the back of a spoon.

Pass through a sieve and pour on top of the rhubarb compote in the espresso cups. Refrigerate for 24 hours.

For the custard

Whisk the egg yolks and sugar together and heat the milk, cream and vanilla pods and seeds on a medium heat. When almost boiling, add to the egg and sugar, whisking continuously and return to the pan. On a low heat, cook the mixture to 87°c or until it coats the back of a spoon and pass the mixture through a sieve.

To assemble and serve

Take six small ramekins, approximately 6cm in diameter, and half fill each with compote, then top with crumble. Bake for 10-15 minutes.

Meanwhile, top the brûlées with a spoon of caster sugar and blow torch until caramelised.

Heat the custard and place in small serving jugs.

Place each component on individual serving dishes with a scoop of ice cream, decorated with edible flowers or small pieces of strawberry.

The Sun Inn
SPLENDOUR

Ye Old Sun Inn at Colton puts Yorkshire produce centre stage.

"We don't buy anything from national companies; it all comes from local producers around York and the Dales," says Ye Old Sun Inn's Ashley McCarthy.

"Using local commodities has always been our ethos; it's not a bandwagon we've jumped on. As a chef, you've got good produce, you don't have to do a lot with it."

Ashley and wife Kelly took over the pub in Colton near York in 2004, and their fresh approach to encourage people in for a pint as well as a meal has paid dividends. The couple, who met while working in a pub together, have picked up a raft of awards including an innovation accolade at The Publican Awards in 2006, the White Rose Yorkshire Pub of the Year, and in 2013, the British Institute of Innkeepers' Licensee of the Year title.

Ye Old Sun Inn concentrates on fresh, seasonal meals, with daily specials and a menu that changes four or five times a year. It also has a mini deli in one of the bars, selling homemade chocolates, jams and flavoured oils.

"Yorkshire to me is diverse, with a wealth of commodities for the chef," says Ashley, who was born in the county but grew up in Lancashire.

"Our venison comes from 10 minutes down the road and the meat is from local farms. The producers are passionate and you share that passion together; they're not just selling a commodity to you."

Inside, the McCarthys have created a destination for food, but where there's also a proper pub atmosphere if you just want to pop in for a pint. The two bars have log burners and a traditional but modern feel, and the large dining room that was added in 2011 is open and airy. There's a bright, modern coffee area too where you can relax with a cuppa and a slice of cake.

The whitewashed 16th century pub is a stone's throw from the A64 and attracts diners and drinkers from York, regular race-goers and visitors from Leeds as well as locals.

"Destination wise, we're easily accessible," said Ashley.

"We're not on the beaten track, but when people know we're here they come to find us."

Ye Old Sun Inn

YE OLD SUN INN BREAD

This is a classic bread recipe that lends itself well to additions of your choice,
such as herbs and seeds to create your own bespoke loaf.
Makes 1kg bread dough – enough for two loaves or 16 individual dinner rolls.

Ingredients

1kg strong bread flour, brown or white

20g table salt

20g dried yeast

30g honey

600ml warm water

Oil for greasing

Feel free to add herbs, seeds or other items to the bread for flavouring

Method

Combine the flour and salt in a large bowl. Make a well in the centre and place to one side.

Mix the yeast and honey into the warm/tepid water and place in a warm area to ferment the yeast and double in size. Make sure your bowl is big enough for it to increase.

Pour the fermented yeast mixture into the well of flour and mix well until all the liquid has been incorporated and the dough is formed.

Tip the dough onto a floured surface and knead until it is satin smooth. Leave to rise for 1 hour until doubled in size or you can put it in the fridge overnight.

Once the dough has risen, knock it back and add any herbs if you're using them, then gently mould into your desired shapes or loaves. Seeds can be added on the crust, just give the dough a light brush of egg white first to ensure they bake onto the bread.

Place onto baking parchment to prove for a further hour until doubled in size.

Heat the oven to 220°c/fan 200°c. Bake for 25-30 minutes for loaves, or 20-25 for the rolls. The timings will vary depending on size of loaves/rolls and oven types.

When it's ready, the bread should be golden brown and sound hollow when tapped underneath.

Cool on a wire rack and enjoy with lots of fresh local butter.

The Home of CHOCOLATE

York's Chocolate Story tells the tale of the sweet stuff's association with the city, with plenty of opportunities to sample the goodies.

Kit Kats, Smarties, Chocolate Oranges and of course, Yorkie bars, all have their roots in York.

Renowned as the home of UK chocolate making, the city's sweet heritage is celebrated at York's Chocolate Story, which tells the tale of why York became – and continues to be – such an important part of our chocolate industry.

Visitors to the attraction can spend a couple of hours immersed in chocolate, discovering where it comes from, how it's transformed into treats and learn about making, tasting and enjoying chocolate.

Chocolate brands including Rowntree's and Terry's and confectioner Craven's are all York companies that grew from family businesses in the city.

"York's chocolate and confectionery companies were founded by three families; Rowntree's, Craven's and Terry's. Each family has a unique and fascinating story to tell," says Ralph Hewitt from York's Chocolate Story.

"Some of the world's most famous brands were developed right here in York and are now known the world over, including Kit Kat, Yorkie, Smarties, Terry's Chocolate Orange and Black Magic."

"You still get the smell of chocolate wafting across the city today," said Ralph.

Six million Kit Kats are made in York everyday and 564 are consumed every second around the world. Some places have really interesting flavours like mascarpone cheese and wasabi.

A wasabi Kit Kat may not be to everyone's taste, but the York Chocolate Story tour will be if you're a fan of the sweet stuff. It tells the tale of chocolate from the Mayans and Aztecs, its arrival in Europe and how it became so important to York and its economy.

"You can try all different varieties and learn to taste like a professional," said Ralph.

Visitors can also try their hand at making their own chocolate lollies to take home, and buy goodies made by the in-house chocolatiers in the café and shop, where there is also a huge selection of different brands.

"A big part of it is keeping the chocolate heritage alive and continuing the story of the people who worked in it," said Ralph.

York's Chocolate Story

RASPBERRY AND ORANGE DARK CHOCOLATE BAR

Make your own chocolate bar at home with this easy guide to creating a tailor-made treat. Makes 1 x 100g bar (adjust the measurements to suit your mould size.)

Ingredients

100g good quality dark chocolate (preferably couverture with no vegetable fat)

3–4 drops raspberry oil

40g candied range pieces or slices

10g freeze dried raspberries, crumbled

Useful equipment for chocolate making:

Bar mould (polycarbonate is best, however silicon can be used) – available from cook shops or online

Piping bag

Plastic bowl

Spatula

Thermometer

Cotton wool

Method

Clean and dry the mould, then polish with cotton wool to stop the chocolate sticking and give a better gloss.

Break up the chocolate into small chunks (or use buttons) and place into the plastic bowl.

Microwave for one minute and stir the chocolate thoroughly. Return to the microwave for 10 second intervals, stirring well in between until the chocolate has a few small lumps remaining. At this point keep stirring, using the residual heat to melt the last few lumps. Use the thermometer to check the chocolate doesn't go over 32°c. Add a few drops of the raspberry oil to taste and mix well.

Pour into a piping bag (use a jug to hold your bag open) and tie or secure with a clip. Cut the tip and pipe the chocolate into your mould until it's just slightly under-filled. Tap the mould on the counter to remove air bubbles and even out the chocolate.

Arrange the orange slices across the bar and sprinkle over the freeze dried raspberries. Ensure your inclusions are all touching chocolate or they won't stick.

Refrigerate for 15-20 minutes to set. Once the chocolate is fully set, give the mould a flex and gently turn out your bar. It should pop out easily but if it isn't quite ready it may need a few more minutes in the fridge. If you're using a silicon mould then carefully loosen the edges and peel away the mould from the chocolate.

Alternatives

Temper some milk chocolate and add orange oil, then put this into a separate piping bag to the raspberry dark chocolate. Pipe half and half into the mould and then use the tip of a knife to swirl the surface of the two chocolates together, creating a marbled effect.

You could also melt down cocoa butter and infuse it with flavours such as chilli flakes, basil leaves, rosemary, lavender, fresh ginger, cardamom etc. Strain the mix through muslin and then add the flavoured cocoa butter to your chocolate for a naturally flavoured bar. Use around 20g of cocoa butter per 100g of chocolate.

Try flavours such as rose, lime, pineapple, mango, caramel, coffee, mint, strawberry, coconut, banana, rhubarb, almond and cherry.

Good inclusions include pistachios, hazelnuts, peanuts, almonds, honeycomb, cereal/biscuit, brownie/toffee pieces, popping candy, jelly sweets, coconut and dried fruits.

The bar will keep for a few weeks depending on the inclusions used.

The DIRECTORY

These great businesses have supported the making of this book; please support and enjoy them.

Amelia's Chocolate
122 Victoria Road,
Scarborough,
North Yorkshire, YO11 1SL
Telephone: 01723 447110
Website: www.ameliaschocolate.co.uk
Handmade chocolates crafted from the best Belgian chocolate, plus chocolate-making workshops for kids and adults.

Ampleforth Abbey Drinks
Ampleforth,
York,
North Yorkshire, YO62 4EY
Telephone: 01439 766778
Website:
www.ampleforthabbeydrinks.org.uk
Cider and juices made from heritage apples in the abbey orchards, plus the only abbey-brewed beer in the UK.

Baltzersen's and Norse
22 Oxford Street,
Harrogate,
North Yorkshire, HG1 1PU
Telephone: 01423 202363
Website: www.baltzersens.co.uk
www.norserestaurant.co.uk
Nordic-inspired café cuisine during the day and fine dining at night, made with Yorkshire ingredients.

Barbakan Café and Restaurant
58 Walmgate,
York,
North Yorkshire, YO1 9TL
Telephone: 01904 672474
Website: www.deli-barbakan.co.uk
Café and restaurant specialising in Eastern European dishes made from North Yorkshire ingredients.

Black Sheep Brewery
Wellgarth,
Masham,
North Yorkshire, HG4 4EN
Telephone: 01765 689227
Website: www.blacksheepbrewery.com
Family owned and run brewery, with visitor centre, bar, shop and bistro.

Bluebird Bakery
5 Talbot Yard Food Court,
Yorkersgate,
Malton,
North Yorkshire, YO17 7FT
Telephone: 07916 324572
Website: www.maltonyorkshire.co.uk/
bluebird-bakery
Real artisan bread and baked goods made using wild yeast and organic flour.

Butter Bees
12 Market Street,
Malton,
North Yorkshire, YO17 7JP
Telephone: 0739 9086209
Website: www.butter-bees.co.uk
Hand-churned organic Yorkshire butter

Cleveland Corner
High Street,
Staithes,
North Yorkshire, TS13 5BH
Telephone: 01947 841117
Website: www.clevelandcorner.co.uk
Two-room bed and breakfast and bistro, specialising in seafood and a menu of seasonal, local produce that changes daily.

Eat Me Café
1 Hanover Road,
Scarborough,
North Yorkshire, YO11 1LS
Telephone: 01723 373256
Website: www.eatmecafé.com
Retro-style community café, serving worldwide flavours with an Asian and Scottish influences and a delectable choice of cakes.

The Fairfax Arms

Main Street,
Gilling East,
York,
North Yorkshire, YO62 4JH
Telephone: 01439 788212
Website: www.thefairfaxarms.co.uk
Historic country pub with a large and varied menu, local real ales and a great selection of wines.

Field & Fawcett Wine Merchants and Delicatessen

The Old Dairy,
Bingley House Farm,
Grimston Bar,
York,
North Yorkshire, YO19 5LA
Telephone: 01904 489073
Website: www.fieldandfawcett.co.uk
Wine merchant stocking more than 800 different wines, plus gins, whiskies and real ales, with adjoinong deli.

Filmore & Union

62a Low Petergate,
York,
North Yorkshire, YO1 7HZ
Telephone: 01904 654123

Filmore & Union

Platform 8,
Station Road,
York,
North Yorkshire, YO24 1AB
Telephone: 01904 634599

Filmore & Union

71 Station Parade,
Harrogate,
North Yorkshire, HG1 1ST
Telephone: 01423 560988

Filmore & Union

66 High Street,
Skipton,
North Yorkshire, BD23 1JJ
Telephone: 01756 700738
Website: www.filmoreandunion.com
Healthy and nutritious seasonal food, cocktail bars and dog friendly policy, all wrapped up in a cool Californian vibe.

Food 2 Remember

4 Talbot Yard Food Court,
Yorkersgate,
Malton,
North Yorkshire, YO17 7FT
Telephone: 01653 696575
Website: www.maltonyorkshire.co.uk/
food-2-remember
Butcher, fishmonger and speciality ready meals made to order.

The George at Wath

Main Street,
Wath,
Ripon,
North Yorkshire, HG4 5EN
Telephone: 01765 641324
Website: www.thegeorgeatwath.co.uk
Restaurant, pub and bed and breakfast accommodation, owned by award-winning young chef Harrison Barraclough with a focus on North Yorkshire flavours.

Gisborough Hall Hotel

Whitby Lane,
Guisborough,
North Yorkshire, TS14 6PT
Telephone: 0344 8799149
Website: www.macdonaldhotels.co.uk/
Gisborough
A mix of traditional and modern, Gisborough Hall is a country house hotel with a restaurant, bar, bistro, and spa.

The Grange Hotel

1 Clifton,
York,
North Yorkshire, YO30 6AA
Telephone: 01904 644744
Website: www.grangehotel.co.uk
Luxury hotel in York city centre, with French brasserie, traditional afternoon teas and private dining facilities.

Grays Court

Chapter House Street,
York,
North Yorkshire, YO1 7JH
Telephone: 01904 612613
Website: www.grayscourtyork.com
Grade I listed building with boutique hotel and restaurant focusing on Yorkshire ingredients and seasonal dishes.

Groovy Moo Ice Cream

3 Talbot Yard Food Court,
Yorkersgate,
Malton,
North Yorkshire, YO17 7FT
Telephone: 01653 228090
Website:
www.facebook.com/groovymoo
Yorkshire-made Italian gelato ice cream, with constantly changing flavours.

Haxby Bakehouse

8 Ryedale Court,
The Village,
Haxby,
York,
North Yorkshire, YO32 3SA
Telephone: 01904 765878
Website: www.haxbybakehouse.co.uk
Artisan real bread maker with on-site deli, which runs full-day bread making courses.

Just Jelly

27 Prospect Field,

High Hawsker,

Whitby,

North Yorkshire, YO22 4LG

Telephone: 07468 497627

Website: www.justjelly.co.uk

A range of artisan jellies to serve with meat and fish dishes.

Le Caveau Restaurant

86 High Street,

Skipton,

North Yorkshire, BD23 1JJ

Telephone: 01756 794274

Website: www.lecaveau.co.uk

Locally sourced ingredients, with a great choice of in-season game, served in a restaurant converted from the town's old jail.

Lockwoods Restaurant

83 North Street,

Ripon,

North Yorkshire, HG4 1DP

Telephone: 01765 607555

Website:

www.lockwoodsrestaurant.co.uk

Family-run restaurant serving seasonal modern British and European dishes.

Masons Yorkshire Gin

9 The Craftyard,

Bedale,

North Yorkshire, DL8 1BZ

Telephone: 01677 426467

Website:

www.masonsyorkshiregin.com

Small batch craft gin made in Yorkshire the traditional way in Original, Yorkshire Tea and Lavender varieties.

no8 bistro and no8 catering

8 Gillygate,

York,

North Yorkshire, YO31 7EQ

Telephone: 01904 653074 (bistro)

07500 060497 (catering)

no8 at the York Art Gallery and the Pavilion Pop Up

York Art Gallery,

Exhibition Square,

York,

North Yorkshire, YO1 7EW

Telephone: 01904 624721

no8 at Merchant Adventurers' Hall

The Merchant Adventurers' Hall,

Fossgate,

York,

North Yorkshire, YO1 9XD

Telephone: 01904 653074

Website: www.no8york.co.uk

York-based bistro, cafés and outside catering serving homemade dishes made from fresh, foraged and local produce.

Passione Della Pasta

1 Talbot Yard Food Court,

Yorkersgate,

Malton,

North Yorkshire, YO17 7LG

Telephone: 01653 699339

Website: www.maltonyorkshire.co.uk/ passione-della-pasta

Authentic Italian fresh pasta and sauces made in North Yorkshire.

The Pheasant Hotel

Harome,

Near Helmsley,

North Yorkshire, YO62 5JG

Telephone: 01439 771241

Website: www.thepheasanthotel.com

Country hotel serving refreshing, elegant dishes with a focus on local ingredients in a relaxed atmosphere.

The Plough Inn

21-23 High Street,

Scalby,

Scarborough,

North Yorkshire, YO13 0PT

Telephone: 01723 362622

Website: www.theploughscalby.co.uk

Cosy and comfortable pub and restaurant with rooms and a menu packed with regional produce.

Quarmby's Delicatessen and Coffee House

Cavenagh House,

The Square,

Sheriff Hutton,

York,

North Yorkshire, YO60 6QX

Telephone: 01347 878779

Website: www.quarmbys.co.uk

Deli and coffee house selling locally sourced ingredients and homemade goodies, teas and coffees.

Quayside Fish and Chips

7 Pier Road,

Whitby,

North Yorkshire, YO21 3PU

Telephone: 01947 825346

Website: www.quaysidewhitby.co.uk

Award-winning sustainable fish and chips from a fourth generation family business, with a cocktail bar and Bram Stoker connection upstairs.

Rafi's Spicebox York

17 Goodramgate,

York,

North Yorkshire, YO1 7LW

Telephone: 01904 430850 (option 2)

Website: www.spicebox.co.uk

Rafi's Spicebox Harrogate
15 Commercial Street,
Harrogate,
North Yorkshire, HG1 1UB
Telephone: 01904 430850 (option 4)
Website: www.spicebox.co.uk
Family business selling quality spices and handmade spice mixes for homemade curries.

Robinsons Café
7 Bishopthorpe Road,
York,
North Yorkshire, YO23 1NA
Email: hello@robinsonscafé.co.uk
Website: www.robinsonscafé.co.uk
Family-run café with tasty choices made from local ingredients, coffees, teas and alcoholic drinks, plus a pre-order homemade ready meals service.

Roost Coffee Roasters
6 Talbot Yard Food Court,
Yorkersgate,
Malton,
North Yorkshire, YO17 7FT
Telephone: 01653 697635
Website: www.roostcoffee.co.uk
Freshly-roasted coffee, espresso bar and mini-tour available.

Rusty Shears Tea Room
4 Silver Street,
Whitby,
North Yorkshire, YO21 3BU
Telephone: 01947 605383
Website: www.facebook.com/Rusty-Shears-350931581712085
A quirky mix of contemporary and vintage, with a huge choice of gins and a great selection of café meals and sharing boards.

The Rythre Arms
Ryther Village,
Near Tadcaster,
North Yorkshire, LS24 9EE
Telephone: 01757 268372
Website: www.rythrearms.co.uk
Family-owned and run steakhouse in a converted pub, specialising in top quality beef.

Skosh
98 Micklegate,
York,
North Yorkshire, YO1 6JX
Telephone: 01904 634849
Website: www.skoshyork.co.uk
Asian-influenced grazing menu, served on small plates in a relaxed atmosphere

Slingsby Gin
5-7 Montpellier Parade,
Harrogate,
North Yorkshire, HG1 2TJ
Telephone: 01423 541279
Website: www.wslingsby.co.uk
Harrogate gin made with water from and specially selected botanicals sourced from the spa town.

Star Inn at Harome
Main Street,
Harome,
Near Helmsley,
North Yorkshire, YO62 5JE
Telephone: 01439 770397
Website: www.thestaratharome.co.uk
Michelin-starred historic thatched inn with a focus on modern Yorkshire cooking, seasonal and locally-sourced ingredients

Visit York
1 Museum Street,
York,
North Yorkshire, YO1 7DT
Telephone: 01904 550099
Website: www.visityork.org
York's official visitor information service.

The Whitby Deli
22-23 Flowergate,
Whitby,
North Yorkshire, YO21 3BA
Telephone: 01947 229062
Website: www.thewhitbydeli.co.uk
Deli selling local and European produce, with own label products and adjoining dining area.

The White Hart Country Inn
Main Street,
Hawes,
North Yorkshire, DL8 3QL
Telephone: 01969 667214
Website:
www.whitehartcountryinn.co.uk
16th century coaching inn set on a cobbled street, with a menu packed with Yorkshire flavours and everything from stock to ice cream made in-house.

Ye Old Sun Inn
Colton,
Tadcaster,
North Yorkshire, LS24 8EP
Telephone: 01904 744261
Website: www.yeoldsuninn.co.uk
16th century whitewashed inn serving meals made from Yorkshire produce, with a mini deli full of homemade goodies in one of the bars.

York's Chocolate Story
King's Square
York,
North Yorkshire, YO1 7LD
Telephone: 01904 527765
Website: www.yorkschocolatestory.com
Tour telling the tale of York's chocolate, with sampling and making opportunities, plus café and shop.

A celebration of the amazing food & drink on our doorstep.

The Essex Cook Book

©2017 Meze Publishing. All rights reserved.

First edition printed in 2017 in the UK.

ISBN: 978-1-910863-25-1

Thank you: Daniel Clifford, Thomas Leatherbarrow

Compiled by: Kelly Markell

Written by: Kate Reeves-Brown

Photography by: Matt Crowder & Tim Green

(www.timgreenphotographer.co.uk)

Edited by: Phil Turner

Designed by: Paul Cocker, Tom Crosby

PR: Kerre Chen, Laura Wolvers

Contributors: Faye Bailey, Katie Fisher,
Sarah Koriba, Anna Tebble

Cover art: Luke Prest (www.lukeprest.com)

Published by Meze Publishing Limited

Unit 1b, 2 Kelham Square

Kelham Riverside

Sheffield S3 8SD

Web: www.mezepublishing.co.uk

Tel: 0114 275 7709

Email: info@mezepublishing.co.uk

CONTENTS

FOREWORD

Having lived in Essex for 12 years before I opened The Flitch of Bacon, I was well aware of the impressive natural larder that exists in the county. I lived just around the corner from the pub, which was derelict at the time, but the inspiration to take it over came when I found myself repeatedly struggling to get a table somewhere for a nice Sunday lunch.

I knew that it would be easy to create dishes from local ingredients here – the beautiful countryside that surrounds us is packed full of farmers producing the best quality meat, fruit and vegetable growers providing seasonal fresh produce, rapeseed growers making lovely British oil, cheese-makers, millers, winemakers, bakers and a whole host of other artisanal producers. And as well as the verdant landscape, we are lucky enough to have a coastline that gives the county access to the freshest fish and shellfish.

The popularity of the thriving and ever-growing Essex Festival of Food and Drink is testament to the passion of people in the county to support local and seasonal produce. A love of food seems to permeate through the entire county. Visiting the festival for me is a chance to meet all the producers, taste their produce and bring it to my menu at The Flitch of Bacon.

Since we opened in December 2015, we have been joined in the area by some other incredible restaurants, which is providing a real boost to the culinary culture of Essex. People here love great food and drink, and they love to support it on their doorstep. As you drive around the countryside here, you can stumble upon countless hidden gems serving up some really delicious dishes.

This book will introduce you to just some of the people and places making Essex one of the country's leading foodie hotspots – and I hope you enjoy trying some of their recipes.

Daniel Clifford – The Flitch of Bacon

WELCOME TO ESSEX

Being a younger chef in this ever-changing world of flavour, passion and flair, I can't talk much of back in the day from first-hand, only what I've picked up and studied along the way. But, as an 'Essex Boy', I can talk with pride about the development and growth of the food scene right here in Essex.

Being an 'Essex boy' myself, I grew up by the seaside full of fish and chips, and seafood alike, spending time fishing with my dad off the beach and laying prawn nets in the rocks to come and collect a few days later. Grandad had a fish and chip shop a stone's throw from the sand. Back then, down by the sea, fish and chips and all those seafood offerings were king.

Away from the sea, there were always a few of those well-renowned restaurants run by families and friends, where the cooking and serving of their food was as though you were part of the family, real cooking from the heart.

So where are we now, you'll ask.

Essex has become a beacon in the UK food industry, with some establishments being at the forefront of gastronomic delight. Celebrity chefs are opening up restaurants to compete with those already flourishing for a Michelin star, as well as other awards, and becoming 'must-visit' destinations.

Not only are there incredibly powerful flavours and food combinations being presented in stunning arrays all over Essex, more so now than ever before, the quality and availability of fresh local produce is unbelievable. Local makers provide restaurants and businesses with a vast range of produce from jams and preserves to sauces and juices, and of course, that marvellous old tipple of chefs, gin! Core ingredients and heritage fruits and vegetables are in abundance right on our doorsteps.

It is time that we 'Essex boys and girls' shout about the offerings we have and show those who are still in the dark about what we can do and just what they are missing out on! This cook book will show off the best of Essex and no doubt the places and chefs to watch too.

For you home cooks, I hope it inspires you to carry on cooking but be bold and adventurous with your flavours and try new things. For all young chefs at college or just starting out, I hope the following pages help to inspire you and get your creative ideas and taste buds blossoming.

Thomas Leatherbarrow

Thomas Leatherbarrow
PEAR, FROMAGE BLANC, VANILLA

Warming spices and heady aromas make this luxurious dish an autumn and winter favourite. The fromage blanc needs to be started the day before.

Preparation time: 2 hours, plus chilling & freezing | Cooking time: 1 hour 30 minutes | Serves 10

Ingredients

For the poached pears:

2 litres red wine

500ml dark aged Port

300ml Madeira

4 cinnamon sticks

10 cloves

5 bay leaves

6 star anise

1.56kg caster sugar

35g sea salt flakes

10 conference pears, peeled

For the vanilla fromage blanc:

500g fromage blanc

3 vanilla pods

145g icing sugar

For the spiced sponge:

40g sweet mixed spice (cinnamon, star anise, mace, cloves, cardamom, allspice, nutmeg)

210g egg whites

80g egg yolks

200g fine caster sugar

90g self-raising flour

For the pear sorbet:

1kg pear purée

700ml water

500g sugar

100ml sorbitol

For the nut and oat crumb:

75g caster sugar

20g hazelnuts

15g walnuts

8g table salt

50g rolled oats

For the pear gel:

400g pear purée

50g caster sugar

6g Ultratex (available online)

For the syrup:

435g caster sugar

Method

For the poached pears

Add all the ingredients except the pears to a large pot and bring to the boil. Boil for 15 minutes, turn down to a simmer, then add the pears. Cover the surface with a round of greaseproof paper and poach for 45 minutes. Remove from the heat and leave to cool in the poaching syrup.

For the vanilla fromage blanc

Hang the fromage blanc in muslin cloth overnight in the fridge. The next day, remove the fromage blanc from the cloth, add to a mixing bowl along with the sugar and scraped vanilla pods. Beat until smooth and then store in the fridge.

For the spiced sponge

Combine all the ingredients in a blender and blitz until smooth. Pass through a fine chinois. (In the kitchen we use a siphon gun to aerate with makes a lighter sponge). Leave to sit for 1½ hours in the fridge. Place into a microwave-safe container or takeaway cup to fill half-way, then microwave on full power for 1 minute 20 seconds.

For the pear sorbet

Bring all the ingredients to the boil in a saucepan and cook out for 6 minutes on a medium heat. Pass through a sieve and chill down in the fridge. Freeze, then churn in an ice cream maker, alternatively, freeze in a container and use a fork to stir every 30 minutes.

For the nut and oat crumb

Preheat the oven to 185°c. Place the sugar in a pan and heat until it has melted and is a light caramel. Do not stir, but swirl the pan occasionally to help the sugar melt. Add all of the nuts and the salt, then remove from the + and allow to cool completely. Blend to a medium-grain texture. Dry-roast the rolled oats in the preheated oven for 11 minutes. Mix the blended caramel nuts with the rolled oats. Store in an air tight container

For the pear gel

Add all the ingredients to a food processor or blender, starting with the purée. Blend on a high speed until smooth and thick. Place the mixture into a squeezy bottle and store in the fridge.

For the syrup

Place the liquid only that you used for cooking the pears back on the heat. Add the sugar and reduce by three-quarters until it is sticky and glossy. Remove from the heat and store in the fridge. Don't worry if it almost sets in the fridge, just take out and heat it gently in the microwave.

To serve

Plate up the pears, fromage blanc, spiced sponge, sorbet, crumb, gel and syrup as shown in the photograph and serve.

Exceptionally ESSEX

At The Anchor Riverside, it's all about working with the seasons to produce outstanding food in a relaxed atmosphere...

Since it opened its doors seven years ago, The Anchor Riverside has become synonymous with fresh, ethically sourced, local produce. Head chef Daniel Watkins has been at the helm since day one, and he has driven this passion for celebrating Essex's natural larder. An Essex boy born and bred, Daniel has been championing the county's produce in his cooking for many years.

As well as featuring in The Good Food Guide 2017, The Anchor Riverside was awarded a Michelin Bib Gourmand in 2016, which it has retained for a second year in 2017. It is the only restaurant in Essex to hold this coveted award, which recognises outstanding food served at moderate prices.

For Daniel, their success is not only down to carefully selecting their ingredients, but also providing a broad range of dining options, from a lunch menu and fixed-price set menu to an extensive evening menu and regularly changing specials. As well as a Sunday menu and children's menu, The Anchor Riverside also offers an impressive vegan menu – which is a real labour of love for Daniel, as a vegan himself.

The menu takes inspiration from around the world, while cleverly putting local Essex ingredients centre stage. This isn't fusion dining by any means, it's creative modern cooking that has its own unique identity. It is all about putting flavour into food – whether that means fermenting their own turmeric to add to curry paste or adding zing to a poached red prawn cocktail with yuzu mayonnaise.

Food of this quality deserves to be enjoyed in a beautiful setting. Thanks to the restaurant's location on the River Crouch, food can be enjoyed in the light and airy orangery, the elegant restaurant or the riverside gardens. The relaxed venue has a brasserie feel with a warmth to the ambience that is maintained by the young and energetic team of staff.

The aim for the future? To continue to produce creative dishes using the best ingredients they can find, to celebrate the incredible natural larder they have on their doorstep and to put the Essex food scene firmly on the country's culinary map.

The Anchor Riverside
GOAT'S CHEESE ESPUMA, HAZELNUT AND MISO BEETROOT

The richness of goat's cheese with the earthy beetroot is a match made in heaven, which is brought together by a smooth hazelnut cream and some crunchy roasted hazelnuts.

Preparation time: 1 hour, plus 1-2 hours chilling | Cooking time: 1 hour | Serves 4-6

Ingredients

For the goat's cheese espuma:

250g soft goat's cheese

125g sour cream

45ml rapeseed oil

1g salt

1g sugar

125g double cream

For the hazelnut cream:

125g toasted hazelnuts

125g raw hazelnuts

350g milk (or use hazelnut milk)

For the beetroot emulsion:

500ml beetroot juice

100ml blackcurrant vinegar or Cabernet Sauvignon vinegar

3 egg yolks

250ml rapeseed oil

Seasoning

For the beetroot:

1 large ruby beetroot

1 large golden beetroot

Rapeseed oil

Splash of vinegar

1 tsp miso

For the garnish:

Roasted hazelnuts

Hazelnut oil

Pickled blackcurrants (pickled in the summer)

Beetroot powder

Method

For the goat's cheese espuma

Place all the ingredients except the double cream into a blender and blend until smooth. Fold in the double cream. Refrigerate for 1–2 hours. For a lighter espuma pass into a siphon canister, charge once and

For the hazelnut cream

Gently heat the ingredients in a saucepan to around 70°c. Remove from the heat and carefully add to a blender, then blitz for 10 minutes (alternatively use a Thermomix if you have one). Set aside with cling film resting on top of the mix and chill.

For the beetroot emulsion

Put the beetroot juice in a pan and reduce it down to 125ml. Add the vinegar and then reduce the mixture to 100ml. Pass the syrup through a sieve and add the egg yolks. Emulsify in a blender with the oil, as you would for a mayonnaise. Season.

For the beetroot

Slice the beetroots finely on a mandoline or Japanese turner, then season and add a little oil, a splash of vinegar and a teaspoon of miso. Vacuum pack them lightly into separate bags and sous vide at 85°c for 25 minutes, then refresh.

For the garnish

The fun bit! Get all the elements ready. I like to fold the beetroot slices in half, like little tacos, with the hazelnut cream in the centre. Place the goat's cheese espuma to the side and finish with the beetroot emulsion, roasted hazelnuts, hazelnut oil, a scattering of the pickled blackcurrants and a dusting of beetroot powder.

The Anchor Riverside
BBQ TURBOT, APPLE, HORSERADISH AND WATERCRESS

This dish showcases a medley of flavours that marry brilliantly – smokiness from the BBQ fish, sweetness from the apple, heat from the horseradish and pepperiness from the watercress.

Preparation time: 45 minutes | Cooking time: 15 minutes | Serves 4-6

Ingredients

For the BBQ turbot:

4-6 turbot fillets, 175g each

Rapeseed oil

Seasoning

For the horseradish emulsion:

1 fresh horseradish, juiced (mind your eyes this will get teary)

100ml rapeseed oil

Good splash of horseradish vinegar

Salt

For the watercress purée:

110g unsalted butter

400g watercress, leaves picked, half of the stalks retained and finely chopped

Salt

200ml chicken or vegetable stock

Beer vinegar or lemon juice, optional

For the compressed apple:

1 apple

Salt

Cider vinegar

To serve:

Lemon juice

Picked watercress leaves

Apple purée

Charred onion

Watercress powder

Watercress oil

Method

For the BBQ turbot

When barbecuing fish, let the barbecue or yakatori grill burn right down so the coals are all white. Brush the fish with rapeseed oil, season and place on the grill. Cook for 5-10 minutes or until cooked to your liking.

For the horseradish emulsion

Place all the ingredients in a high-powered blender and blitz until emulsified.

For the watercress purée

Heat the butter in a pan over a moderate heat. Add the watercress stalks and season well with salt. Cook for 2-3 minutes, until softened, then add the chicken or vegetable stock and the watercress leaves. Cook for 1 minute, until the watercress leaves have just wilted.

Transfer to a food processor and blend until smooth. Pass the purée through a fine sieve into a bowl set over ice, then refrigerate. Check the seasoning (you can add a splash of beer vinegar or lemon juice) and warm through before serving.

For the compressed apple

Baton or dice the apple, and add a little salt and cider vinegar. I compress it on a high setting using a Vacpac machine. Alternatively, at home, you can simply toss the fresh apple in a little salt and vinegar.

To serve

I like to finish the turbot with lemon juice. Spoon the watercress purée on to the plate and dress with picked watercress leaves and the horseradish emulsion. Place the fish to the side and add apple purée.

Dining DESTINATION

From lunch to dinner and right through to evening drinks, Boadicea is a destination bar and restaurant in historic Colchester.

Not many restaurants manage to transition smoothly throughout the day, from laid-back lunches to elegant evening dinners, but Boadicea has achieved this to perfection. Situated outside the centre of Colchester, Boadicea makes the most of its neighbourhood location to welcome locals along with diners who have travelled from further afield to enjoy their evening at this Haven Road gem.

Owner Josh Campbell-Broome opened Boadicea in October 2016, his first solo venture having worked in the hospitality industry for many years. His aim was to create somewhere where people could relax and enjoy their whole evening. No rushing to leave the table, and no need to move on somewhere else after dinner.

The menu is predominantly British with a modern twist, and a few hints of international inspiration dotted throughout. At lunch time, people tuck into sandwiches (think smoked salmon bagel, BLT, pulled pork sandwich or roasted Mediterranean veggies with mozzarella), salads, homemade soup or a ploughman's. Or for hungrier diners, there are also lunch time mains such as steaks, fish, risotto, pasta or handmade burgers (including a vegan courgette falafel burger, alongside beef and chicken burgers).

The evening menu retains the main course lunch options but also evolves to include more sophisticated dining, with dishes such as glazed duck, pork in ginger ale, sea bass or blackened chicken. The food is accompanied by a carefully selected wine list and a good choice of beers. Josh selects the wine list with the help of a specialist each season – a task he admits is one of his favourites!

After dinner, Boadicea transitions subtly into a laid-back bar atmosphere. Each weekend offers something a little different, though the stylish and relaxed vibes remain the same each week. Live music is popular, with jazz being a firm favourite as saxophonists create a chilled-out feel in the bar. There are also seasonal events, along with arty nights, live lounge evenings and DJs.

As it celebrated its first birthday in October 2017, Boadicea is looking to the future – and we can expect plenty more great food, great drinks and great music from this unique destination.

Boadicea
DUCK, BUTTERNUT SQUASH, QUINCE, GINGER

Succulent duck breast coated in gingerbread crumb, crispy duck bon bons, smooth squash purée and tasty pickled squash are all served with an aromatic duck sauce – an impressive dish to try at home.

Preparation time: 1 hour, plus pickling overnight | Cooking time: 3-4 hours | Serves 4

Ingredients

For the duck:

1 whole duck, broken down to legs and breasts

2 star anise

1 garlic clove, crushed, skin on

1 bay leaf

Duck fat, enough to cover the legs

Maldon sea salt

Oil, for deep frying

For the gingerbread crumb:

500g sourdough

50g stem ginger

15g walnuts

20ml rapeseed oil

For the squash:

1 whole squash

1 shallot, finely diced

70ml chicken stock

30ml double cream

500ml pickling liquor

Oil, for frying

For the duck sauce:

2 star anise

1 tsp honey

10g stem ginger

1 clove garlic

600ml chicken stock

To serve:

Quince jelly, cut into 1cm dice

Micro coriander

Method

For the duck

Preheat the oven to 150°c. Place the duck legs in a tray with the anise, garlic and bay leaf. Cover in duck fat and cook in the oven for 2½ hours. Take the duck out of the fat and let cool slightly, then finely pick. Add a little of the duck fat to help set the bon bons, then roll the duck into balls and place in the fridge to set. Score the duck breast ready to cook and set aside.

For the gingerbread crumb

Preheat the oven to 170°c. Blend all the ingredients together to make a crumb, then use half to coat the duck bon bons. Bake the other half in the oven until golden, turning every few minutes. Set aside for later.

For the squash

Cut off the neck of the squash and set aside for pickling. Peel and medium dice the rest of the squash. Fry the shallots in a little oil until soft. Add the diced squash and fry for a further 5 minutes, then add the chicken stock. Cook for 10 minutes until soft, then blend while adding cream until you get the desired consistency. Keep warm.

Cut the reserved squash for pickling into rectangles, then use a peeler to peel it into strips. Add to the pickling liquor and leave overnight.

For the duck sauce

Put all the ingredients into a pan and reduce until it coats the back of a spoon. Strain and set aside.

To serve

Score the duck breasts and season with Maldon sea salt. Add to a cold pan, then turn on the heat and render the fat down, draining the fat from the pan, when needed. Turn the breasts over and seal flesh-side down. Turn the duck back over and flash in a hot oven for 5 minutes, being sure not to overcook. Allow the duck breasts to rest, then trim and place a little sauce on the skin to stick on the ginger crumb. Slice into two. Deep-fry the bon bons for 3 minutes. Place the squash purée on the plate, then add the duck. Garnish with the quince and pickled squash. Finish with micro coriander and duck sauce.

Boadicea
APPLE AND BLACKBERRY CRUMBLE

A classic winter warmer elegantly reinvented with poached blackberries, blackberry sorbet, roasted apples and a blackberry gel. Blackberry purée is available at good supermarkets.

Preparation time: 1 hour, plus freezing & setting| Cooking time: 1 hour | Serves 4

Ingredients

For the poached blackberries:

150g water

100g caster sugar

1 punnet blackberries

For the crumble:

200g caster sugar

200g plain flour

200g unsalted butter

100g oats

1 tbsp honey

For the blackberry sorbet:

250g blackberry purée

185ml water

130g sugar

For the roasted apples:

2 Granny Smith apples

50g butter

50g sugar

For the blackberry fluid gel:

500g blackberry purée

5g agar (available at health food stores)

For the blackberry cream:

3 gelatine sheets

400g double cream

200g blackberry purée

50g sugar

Method

For the poached blackberries

Bring water and sugar to the boil in a pan, then take off the heat. Add the blackberries and leave to cool.

For the crumble

Preheat the oven to 170˚c. Mix the sugar, flour and butter together until the mixture resembles breadcrumbs, then mix in the oats and honey. Bake in the oven for 5 minutes, then mix and repeat until golden all over.

For the blackberry sorbet

Mix the ingredients together, put in an ice cream churner and churn until set. Place in the freezer.

For the roasted apples

Peel and core the apples, then slice to make wedges. Place a pan on the heat, add the butter and heat until it starts to foam. Add the sugar and apple, and cook until caramelised.

For the blackberry fluid gel

Place the purée and agar in a pan and heat to 85˚c. Hold at this heat for 2 minutes to allow the to agar react, then place on a plate in the fridge to set for 20 minutes. Blend until smooth and glossy, then put in a piping bag.

For the blackberry cream

Soak the gelatine in cold water to soften. Put the rest of the ingredients in a pan to warm up, then add the softened gelatine mix. Transfer to a cling film-lined tray, and leave to set for 1 hour. Dice ready for serving.

To serve

Plate up the dish as shown in the picture.

Best of
BRITISH BEEF

A much-loved family business, Deersbrook Farm produces traditional grass-fed beef that is known for its exquisite flavour.

Set within the beautiful Essex countryside, Deersbrook Farm is owned by third-generation farmers Philip and Anna Blumfield, with the help of the fourth generation, their children Oliver and Amber.

The verdant landscape is home to their Native Sussex cattle, who graze year-round on the luscious pastures. It is this idyllic lifestyle that sets their beef apart from other producers – cattle that are 100% grass-fed not only have a superior taste, but are nutritionally better, too. The deep plum colour with its characteristic rich yellow marbling testifies to the premium conditions of the cattle. In fact, the creamy yellow fat signifies that the meat contains less fat and more vitamins and minerals than grain-fed beef.

"We choose the Sussex breed because they thrive on pasture alone, they have a docile nature and fine-textured meat. Sussex beef is well known for its superior eating quality," explains Anna.

Deersbrook Farm is the only Pasture for Life-certified farm in Essex, making its product unique in the county – and it has accumulated many fans. "People who taste our beef for the first time comment that it tastes like 'real beef'," Anna explains. "The traditional farming methods allow us to produce that traditional taste." This is also thanks to them dry-aging all the beef on the bone for 28 days to allow the flavour and texture to develop.

"The way we farm is not only better for the cattle, but for the environment too." From rotating the fields, using their manure and nurturing the local wildlife, they take a comprehensive and long-term approach to farming to ensure success for the future.

Anna is committed to sharing her farm-to-fork passion with the community. As well as opening the farm once a year for Open Farm Sunday, she also visits schools to talk to children about food and farming: "The children absolutely love meeting the rare breed pigs and ask so many questions. They are full of pride when they dig up their potatoes to cook, that they have previously chitted, planted and watered, or cook the meatballs they have prepared."

They supply many restaurants in Essex, such as The Norton, who feature their grass-fed beef on the menu. For home cooks who want to sample the same quality beef as local chefs, Deersbrook Farm beef is available to buy straight from the farm every Friday, as well as from the many farmers' markets Philip and Anna attend. They hope to expand and develop their on-site farm shop in the future – making Deersbrook Farm beef accessible to many more people across the county.

Deersbrook Farm

Native Grass fed Beef

Farm to Fork Friday!

OPEN

9.30 - 6.30pm

Deersbrook Farm
BRAISED SHORT RIB, SAUTÉED KALE, CREAM OF MASHED POTATOES AND RED WINE JUS

A classic combination of flavours that is accentuated with the wonderful taste
and texture of Deersbrook Farm short rib.
This fabulous recipe is by chef Dereck Mhone at The Norton in Cold Norton.

Preparation time: 15 minutes | Cooking time: 2 hours | Serves 2

Ingredients

For the short rib:

1kg Deersbrook Farm short rib

2 celery sticks, chopped

2 cloves garlic, chopped

350ml red wine

2 bay leaves

2 star anise

1 tbsp dark brown sugar

4 sprigs of thyme

Beef stock, to cover

Salt and pepper

For the mashed potatoes:

4 potatoes, peeled and quartered

40ml double cream

40g butter

Salt and pepper

For the sautéed kale:

200g kale

Olive oil, for cooking

Salt and pepper

Method

For the short rib

Preheat the oven to 160°c. Seal the short rib in a hot pan to colour, then transfer to a deep oven tray. In the same pan, add the celery, garlic and red wine and sauté to release the flavours. Once softened, add the mixture to the short rib in the oven tray. Add the bay leaves, star anise, salt and pepper, dark brown sugar, thyme and beef stock to the oven tray to cover the short rib. Cover with baking parchment, then foil, and place in the preheated oven for 2 hours.

For the mashed potatoes

Place the potatoes in a pan and cover with water. Add 1 teaspoon of salt, bring to the boil and simmer until the potato is cooked. Drain the water then mash the potatoes with a ricer. Put the mash into a bowl, add the cream and butter, and bind with a spatula. Season with pepper to taste.

For the sautéed kale

Sauté the kale on low heat with olive oil and seasoning until cooked, but still retaining the crunch – don't overcook it.

To finish and serve

Remove the short rib from the braising liquor and set aside. Strain the braising liquor into a saucepan and reduce by one-third or until slightly thick. There you have your jus. Serve the short rib with the mashed potatoes, sautéed kale and red wine jus.

From soil
TO OIL

Grown, pressed and bottled on a family farm on the Essex/Hertfordshire border, Duchess Oil is a premium British rapeseed oil that is used in some of the country's most famous kitchens.

A sixth-generation family farm, Duchess Farm has seen many changes over its history, from its origins as a dairy farm to today producing award-winning rapeseed oil. Although the farm has been around for generations, the story of Duchess Oil began during the 2012 harvest, when Oscar Harding decided to do things a little differently.

Crop prices were sky-high and he began wondering what happened to their harvest when it left the farm… Farms all over the country were diversifying in order to keep afloat, so Oscar began a little research.

He began by visiting another British producer to learn about the cold-pressing process, and soon he was sending his Duchess rapeseed to be pressed and bottled there. By 2014, Oscar had created the facilities on the farm to cold-press, bottle and label his own oil on-site.

The business took the name of his great grandmother, who was fondly known as Duchess – a nod to the importance of celebrating tradition alongside modern techniques.

Although Duchess Oil is available to buy in shops, Oscar has become a famous face amongst chefs. "Chefs really care about the provenance and quality of their produce," Oscar explains, "and they will often come and visit the farm to learn about how we make it."

One of his favourite customers is Jamie Oliver's Fifteen. Duchess Farms has become a regular field trip for students at the academy there. Another turning point for Duchess Oils was when it began being used at The Ledbury in Notting Hill, a two Michelin-star restaurant known for being one of the world's finest. Oscar describes it as almost the 'stamp of approval' that saw the name Duchess Oil becoming synonymous with fine cuisine.

So, what makes the oil such a favourite amongst those in the know? "This is a first-press oil, and the extraction rate is only around 40%, compared with up to 90% in mass-produced oils. It is also naturally filtered, so there is really very little human involvement. We also make it pretty much to order, so this means it is always fresh – no bottles sit around on shelves waiting for customers."

From growing the crops to pressing and filtering, everything is done slowly and carefully – it takes time to create a great product, and Oscar doesn't plan on changing the way they have always done things any time soon.

Duchess Oil
ORANGE, RAPESEED OIL AND POLENTA CAKE

Rapeseed oil works perfectly in baking. This recipe highlights the sunshine colour of the natural oil, also using oranges and polenta to contribute to this beautiful cake which evokes the colour of the rapeseed fields of the Essex countryside in early summer, combined with the flavours of the Mediterranean.

Preparation time: 10 minutes | Cooking time: 1 hour | Serves 6-8

Ingredients

For the cake:

250g caster sugar

3 eggs

250g fine ground polenta

1 tsp baking powder

Pinch of salt

120ml good-quality orange juice

120ml cold-pressed extra-virgin rapeseed oil

2 oranges, zested

1 tsp vanilla extract

1 tsp orange extract (optional)

For the syrup:

100g caster sugar

4 cardamom pods

75ml water

1 orange, zest in large pieces

For the icing (optional):

200g icing sugar

2 tbsp orange juice

For the decoration:

Orange slices, orange zest or candied orange peel

Method

Preheat the oven to 180°c and prepare a 20cm cake tin by brushing it with oil and lining with parchment paper.

Place the caster sugar and eggs into a large bowl and use an electric whisk or stand mixer to beat them together for about 3 minutes until the mixture is pale yellow, thick and creamy.

In another bowl measure out the polenta and mix in the baking powder and a pinch of salt. If you can't find fine-ground polenta, you can whizz it in a food processor to get a finer grain, which will improve the texture of the finished cake.

In a measuring jug place the orange juice, rapeseed oil, orange zest, vanilla extract and orange extract (if using). Whisk thoroughly until the mixture is well combined.

Fold half of the polenta mixture into the egg mix, then add half of the orange and oil mixture. Repeat, folding carefully between each addition to make sure the ingredients are well combined whilst keeping the mixture as light and airy as possible.

Pour the batter into the prepared tin and bake in the preheated oven for 30 minutes until the cake is golden brown, shrinking away from the edges of the tin and a skewer inserted into the centre comes out clean.

Whilst the cake is baking, prepare the orange and cardamom syrup. Place the caster sugar, cardamom pods and water into a small pan and bring to the boil. Peel large pieces of zest from an orange and add to the pan. Reduce to a simmer and allow to bubble away for a further 10 minutes. Set aside.

When the cake comes out of the oven, and whilst it is still in the tin and warm, use a fine skewer to poke holes all over the cake. Then slowly drizzle over 5-6 tablespoons of the syrup, allowing it to trickle through the cake. Keep any further syrup aside as an extra garnish when serving.

The icing is optional, but makes a lovely finish to the cake. Sift the icing sugar into a small bowl and then squeeze one of the zested oranges to get 2-3 tablespoons of juice from it. Mix this into the icing sugar to form a smooth glacé icing, which is thick enough to coat the back of a spoon but will still drizzle down the sides of the cake. Finally, decorate the cake with some orange slices, extra orange zest grated on top or some candied orange peel, and serve.

Duchess Oil
GARLIC, FENNEL AND ROSEMARY ROAST POTATOES

These delicious roast potatoes are perfectly cooked in golden rapeseed oil, which gives a fabulous crispy and golden-brown finish. Ever since I discovered rapeseed oil, I wouldn't use anything else to roast my potatoes. The added flavourings of garlic, fennel and rosemary really add to the natural flavour of potato, and the mild fennel flavour makes this recipe a particularly good accompaniment for roast pork. Maris Pipers or King Edwards work perfectly in this recipe, but any floury potato is good for roasting.

Preparation time: 10 minutes | Cooking time: 1 hour | Serves 4 as a side dish

Ingredients

1kg Maris Piper or King Edward potatoes

60ml cold-pressed extra-virgin rapeseed oil

2 tsp fennel seeds

6 garlic cloves, unpeeled and lightly crushed

2 sprigs of fresh rosemary, finely chopped

Salt

Method

Peel the potatoes and cut them into large chunks (around 5-6cm wide). Place them into a large pan of cold water and add a generous pinch of salt.

Preheat the oven to 220°c (200°c fan).

Place the pan on the heat and bring the water to a boil. Reduce the heat to a simmer and allow the potatoes to cook for 8-10 minutes. Then drain the potatoes into a colander and allow them to steam dry for a minute or two.

Once they are dry, give them a good toss around in the colander to rough up the edges of the potatoes. Do this carefully; you don't want to break them up completely.

Take a metal roasting tin or baking tray with a raised edge, add the extra-virgin rapeseed oil and place the tin into the oven to preheat for 5 minutes.

Carefully remove the tin, remembering the oil will be hot. Add the fennel seeds and garlic cloves to the oil which should sizzle slightly. Then add the parboiled potatoes to the hot pan. Scatter over the chopped rosemary and season with sea salt. Use two spoons to turn the potatoes over until they are well-coated in the golden oil.

Return the roasting pan to the oven and roast for 40-45 minutes, depending on how golden-brown you like your potatoes. Turn the potatoes over with the two spoons or tongs half way through the cooking time.

The perfect pub
EXPERIENCE

A relaxed environment, great food and drink, and friendly service are the order of the day at The Eight Bells, one of Saffron Walden's most charming historic pubs.

When Leanne and Paul Cutsforth of Primavera Pubs took over The Eight Bells in 2011, they knew exactly what they wanted to achieve in the ancient building. For Leanne, who admits that hospitality runs in her blood, one of her greatest pleasures in life is enjoying good food and wine with good company gathered around the table, and it is something she worked hard to bring to The Eight Bells.

She maintained the exterior of the stunning barn (one of the oldest buildings in Saffron Walden) as traditionally as possible, while working with the character of the interior to create a warm and cosy environment that would welcome people in. Cosy Chesterfield sofas, overflowing bookshelves, roaring log fires and exposed timber create an irresistible ambience under the rafters of the old barn.

Just a year after opening, David Webb became head chef, and he has now been heading up the kitchen for five years. His focus on fresh and seasonal produce is evident in the menu, from the pub classics (such as locally sourced sausages with mash) to the regularly changing specials, which often include ingredients from his own garden or the neighbouring allotments. When it comes to the specials, David loves to allow the chefs some creative freedom to explore new ideas.

His love of food started early in life with an appreciation of Mediterranean flavours. This passion shines in his dishes, where bursts of vibrancy and bold flavours give his food a certain oomph. Out of the kitchen, his other passion is his well-tended garden. He will often use home-grown herbs and edible flowers in his cooking, especially those things that are more unusual. He uses his salad burnet (a herb that tastes like cucumber) in a seasonal mackerel dish and finishes the odd special with edible flowers, such as nasturtium or borage.

There are very few things not made by hand in the kitchen, so for the occasional item sourced from other suppliers, they insist on the best – for example, award-winning ice cream from Saffron Ice Cream Company, which is made on a family farm nearby and is the perfect way to finish off a meal at The Eight Bells.

The Eight Bells
PAN-ROASTED LOIN OF HAKE, LOCAL SAFFRON RISOTTO AND CUMBRIAN HAM CRISP

This vibrant hake dish never fails to make an appearance on the menu,
here at The Eight Bells, from late spring through late summer.
With the addition of locally produced saffron from David Smale, it puts
a little piece of Essex heritage into a Mediterranean-inspired dish.

Preparation time: 35 minutes, soak the saffron the night before | Cooking time: 30 minutes | Serves 4

Ingredients

For the ham crisps:

4 slices Woodalls Cumbrian ham

For the risotto base:

40g unsalted butter

1 banana shallot, thinly sliced

1 rosemary stalk, leaves reserved

200g Carnaroli risotto rice

150ml white wine

400ml good-quality chicken stock

To finish the risotto:

200ml chicken stock

50g picante cooking chorizo, pre-cooked and very finely diced

50g piquillo peppers, thinly sliced

1g fresh rosemary, finely chopped

12 saffron threads, soaked in 4 tbsp water for 24 hours

30g fresh shelled peas

30g courgette, very finely diced

30g fresh double-shelled broad beans

30g mangetout, thinly sliced

40g unsalted butter

70g Parmesan, freshly grated

Maldon sea salt and black pepper, to taste

For the hake:

4 hake loin fillets, 150g each

Rapeseed oil and butter, for cooking

To serve:

Chive oil

Garlic chives

Method

For the ham crisps

Preheat the oven to 120°c. Place the ham between two sheets of parchment paper on a flat baking sheet and place another baking sheet on top. Dehydrate in the oven for 15-20 minutes. This can be done in advance and stored in an airtight container.

For the risotto base

Melt the butter in a pan over a very low heat. Add the shallot and rosemary stalk. Soften without colour; 3-5 minutes. Add the rice and stir to coat. Add the white wine and cook until absorbed. Add the chicken stock and bring to a gentle simmer, stir only once or twice to separate the grains. Leave on a gentle simmer until the stock has been absorbed and the rice is three-quarters cooked. Not stirring the rice during this process helps to develop the starch, which gives the finished risotto its silky texture. At this point, the risotto base can be chilled until required, or continue to the next stage.

To finish the risotto

You will need to time this around the cooking of your hake. Preheat the oven to 160°c. Bring the chicken stock to a simmer. Add the chorizo, piquillo peppers and rosemary, cook for 1-2 minutes and then add the risotto base. Bring back up to a simmer and add the saffron infusion and fresh peas. Cook for 3-4 minutes; you can stir the risotto as often as required at this stage, as the starch has already developed. Add the courgette and broad beans, and cook for a further 3-4 minutes. The risotto should still be quite loose at this stage. If not, add a little more chicken stock or water. Add the mangetout and cook for 2 minutes. Add the butter and incorporate, followed by the Parmesan. Once the Parmesan has incorporated fully, season with salt and pepper. Remove from the heat. Rest the risotto in a warm place while you cook the fish.

For the hake

Place an oven-safe frying pan large enough to hold the hake fillets over a medium-high heat. Line with parchment paper, and drizzle in some rapeseed oil. Once the pan is nice and hot, add the hake fillets skin-side down. Cook without disturbing for 2-3 minutes, until the skin is crisp and golden. Place a knob of butter on each fillet, and season with Maldon sea salt. Place in the preheated oven and cook for 4 minutes more, until cooked (depending on your oven). Remove from the oven and flip the hake over onto its flesh side. Rest the fish in the pan while you plate the risotto.

To serve

Divide the risotto between four warm plates. Place the hake in the centre and season the skin with a few sea salt flakes. Add a ham crisp to the left side of the hake, scatter with the garlic chives, and drizzle the chive oil around the risotto. Serve immediately.

The Flitch of Bacon
BASS, SCALLOPS, BOUILLIBAISSE

The Flitch of Bacon is a restaurant with a long history. Daniel Clifford is the chef behind its exciting new chapter. A relaxed atmosphere allows diners to enjoy inspiring seasonal food in a charming dining environment. Set within the beautiful Essex countryside in Little Dunmow, guests can also take advantage of its three guest rooms and luxurious breakfast.

Preparation time: 1 hour | Cooking time: 1 hour | Serves 1

Ingredients

For the bass:

90g portion of bass fillet

For the scallop:

1 scallop

For the bouillabaise:

1 onion, roughly chopped

1 carrot, roughly chopped

1 leek, roughly chopped

2 sticks celery, roughly chopped

1 fennel bulb, roughly chopped

1kg fish bones

2 tbsp tomato purée

1 tsp fennel seeds

1 star anise

50ml Pernod

50ml brandy

Lemon, to infuse

Tarragon, to infuse

50g butter

Splash of skimmed milk

For the rouille:

½ garlic clove

4 red piquillo peppers

2 egg yolks

1 tsp lemon juice

Pinch of saffron

250ml extra-virgin olive oil

Method

For the bass

Score the skin on the bass fillet.

For the scallops

Open the scallop and set aside.

For the bouillabaisse

Roast the vegetables until golden, add the fish bones and tomato purée, then add the fennel seeds and star anise, and deglaze with the alcohol. Cover with water, bring to the boil and skim. Simmer for 1 hour, turn up the heat, infuse with lemon and tarragon. Strain through a muslin, then reduce. Add the butter and a splash of skimmed milk, then blend with a hand blender.

For the rouille

Blend all the ingredients together slowly until they emulsify. Season.

To serve

Sear the bass and scallops in a hot pan. Finish with a squeeze of lemon on the top. Transfer to a plate and dot the rouille on the side. Pour the bouillabaisse over. We serve this with saffron potatoes and fennel. Dress the plate with baby basil, dill, olive oil, espelette, Nocellara olives and tomato confit.

Perfect POULTRY

Third-generation family business, Great Clerkes Farm Foods, has been rearing healthy and happy free-range chickens, geese, guinea fowl, turkeys and ducks since the end of the Second World War.

Great Clerkes Farm is run by Simon Hughes in the picturesque location of Little Sampford, just outside the historic town of Thaxted. Hidden down a long country lane, the farm enjoys a beautiful setting amidst Essex's rural landscape.

Simon is the third generation of his family to take over the running of the farm. It was started by his grandfather Henry Brian Hughes, who was followed by Simon's father Paddy and his mother Stephanie. Today Simon and his wife Clare rear thousands of poultry each year using free-range farming methods to the highest welfare standards. They are helped by the farm's best-loved family member Morph the dog, a famous face around Great Clerkes Farm.

The landscape makes the perfect home for free-range poultry – the rich grassland is dotted with fruit trees, and the scrubland provides the ideal environment for the birds to roam and feed freely throughout the warmer months.

Throughout the year, they rear 1000 chickens and 500 ducks, as well as turkeys, guinea fowl and a staggering 1200 geese for Christmas. Give them a call or send them an email to order one for your Christmas dinner. They also supply many local butchers and farm shops, and have a website from which you can order, if you can't get to the farm to buy directly – although it's worth a trip to enjoy the picturesque scenery of this hidden haven.

During the summer, Great Clerkes Farm takes full advantage of its pretty gardens with pop-up restaurants that take place on the lawn of the farm house. Head chef Jack Barnett makes use of the varied produce grown on the farm (not just the free-range poultry, but the vegetables and fruits that are also grown by the family) to prepare a seasonally inspired menu.

From al fresco summer dining to festive free-range birds, Great Clerkes Farm Food embraces the changing seasons to celebrate the very best of Essex produce in its beautiful rural setting.

Great Clerkes Farm
FREE-RANGE ROAST GOOSE WITH CITRUS

I chose this recipe because any fruit is a perfect accompaniment to the unique flavour of a goose, but the citrus really complements it well. It is also the best combination when you have an apple or apricot stuffing alongside.

Preparation time: 20 minutes | Cooking time: 2-2½ hours| Serves 8-10

Ingredients

1 goose, approximately 5.5kg

4 lemons

3 limes

1 tsp five-spice

Small handful parsley

Small handful thyme, plus extra leaves for sprinkling

Small handful sage

3 tbsp honey

Oil, for browning

Sea salt and black pepper

Method

Using the tip of a sharp knife, lightly score the breast and leg skin of the goose in a criss-cross pattern. This helps the fat to render down more quickly during roasting.

Grate the zest from the lemons and limes, and reserve the zested fruits. Mix the lemon and lime zest with 2 teaspoons fine sea salt, the five-spice powder and pepper to taste. Season the cavity of the goose generously with salt, then rub the citrus zest well into the skin and sprinkle some inside the cavity.

Stuff the zested fruit and the parsley, thyme and sage inside the bird and set aside for at least 15 minutes. This can be done up to a day ahead and kept refrigerated.

Preheat the oven to 240°c/220°c fan/gas 9. If you want to give the bird a nice golden skin, brown it in a large frying pan (or a heavy-based roasting tin), using a couple of tablespoons of oil. Holding the bird by the legs (you may like to use an oven glove), press it down on the breasts to brown.

Once browned, place the bird in the roasting tin. Drizzle with the honey and sprinkle with the extra thyme leaves. Cook for 10 minutes, then reduce the oven temperature to 190°c/170°c fan/gas 5 and cook for 20 minutes per kg for medium-rare, 30 minutes per kg for more well-done, plus 30 minutes resting. Cover the goose with foil if it is starting to brown too much. Every 30 minutes or so, baste the bird with the pan juices, then pour off the fat through a sieve into a large heatproof bowl. You will end up with at least a litre of luscious fat – save this for the potatoes and other veg.

At the end of the cooking time, leave the goose to rest for at least 30 minutes, covered loosely with foil. The bird will not go cold, but will be moist and much easier to carve.

All about THE TASTE

Great Garnetts has been producing high-quality pork and turkey, on the family farm since 1970 – totally traceable, totally delicious.

Great Garnetts supply pork to some of the best kitchens in Essex – you'll see their award-winning sausages, pork, gammon and bacon on menus in a plethora of pubs, restaurants and cafés in the county.

So, what makes the pork at Great Garnetts so deliciously different to other pork on the market? For owner Jonathan, it is all about the carefully selected breeds and the top-quality feed they choose. Their herd is housed on deep beds of straw and fed locally milled food, which is available for the pigs to eat and drink as they wish.

Jonathan took over the farm from his father, who started the business in 1970. Today a team of three stockmen is headed up by Robert Perry, who has over 20 years' experience. In 2000, Jonathan decided to expand the business to include butchery, too. This meant that the meat was back from the local abattoir on the same day, ready to be prepared on the premises.

"All fresh joints are craft-butchered and tied with string, all sausages are linked by hand and all bacon is dry-cured. Smoking takes place in an old brick smokehouse where the meat is hung over smouldering oak and beech chips," explains Jonathan.

The hard work in animal husbandry and butchery has paid off with a haul of Great Taste Awards for their pork, turkey and gammon.

The farm shop is open on Thursday afternoons and Friday mornings for people to pick up their bacon and sausages for a weekend breakfast or a joint of pork for Sunday dinner perhaps. However, for those who can't make it to the farm, there is also an easy-to-use online shop.

On the second Saturday of the month (with the exceptions of August and December), Great Garnetts hosts a popular farmers' market in their impressive 15th-century barn, where their produce is available alongside an array of other local producers, crafts and refreshments. There is always so much to see and do; the farmers' market is one of the family's greatest pleasures, as it brings the community together through a love of local produce.

As Christmas approaches, Great Garnetts become just as well-known for their turkeys as they are for their famous pork. Just like with the pork, commitment to welfare and quality has led to them rearing traditional, slow-growing breeds – and with a Great Taste Award to their name, you can be sure they will make Christmas dinner extra special.

Visit their online shop at www.greatgarnetts.co.uk

Great Garnetts
BAKED HAM

Here we share our Great Garnetts secret to preparing the perfect gammon.

Preparation time: 10 minutes | Cooking time: 1-2 hours | Serves 8

Ingredients

2kg piece of gammon

1 onion, halved

1 carrot, halved

1 celery stick, halved

1 bouquet garni

6 peppercorns

For the glaze:

Mustard, for brushing

Cloves, for studding

Brown sugar, for sprinkling

Method

Place the gammon in a large pan and cover with water. Bring slowly to the boil and then drain.

Add the onion, carrot, stick of celery, bouquet garni and peppercorns. Cover again with water and bring to the boil.

Continue to cook for 10 minutes per 450g plus a further 10 minutes (approx. 50 minutes for a 2kg piece of gammon).

Meanwhile, preheat the oven to 180°c.

Remove the gammon from the water and take off the skin. Score the fat in diamonds using a sharp knife. Place the joint on a baking tray and spread a thin layer of mustard over the ham. Stud it with cloves and sprinkle with brown sugar. Bake in the preheated oven for 30 minutes.

This baked ham is delicious served hot or cold.

Great Garnetts
NORMANDY PORK CASSEROLE

This is a French-inspired casserole that makes the most of high-welfare, Great Garnetts pork. It is simple to make at home but never fails to impress thanks to its rich flavours.

Preparation time: 15 minutes | Cooking time: 2 hours 30 minutes | Serves 6

Ingredients

55g butter

1kg diced pork

200g streaky bacon, roughly chopped, or lardons

1 small onion, chopped

2 celery sticks, chopped

285ml dry cider

285ml chicken stock

6 tbsp half-fat crème fraiche

2 tbsp cornflour mixed with 2 tbsp water

2 tbsp Dijon mustard

2 tbsp tarragon leaves

Method

Preheat the oven to 170°c. Place a large pan over a medium heat and add the butter. Add the pork, in batches, and fry until browned all over. Remove from the pan and set aside.

Dry-fry the chopped bacon or lardons, then remove and set aside.

Add the chopped onion and celery to the pan and cook gently until softened. Add the pork and lardons back into the pan, pour over the cider and chicken stock, cover and cook for 2 hours.

After 2 hours, add the remaining ingredients and continue to cook on the hob, stirring regularly, until the sauce has thickened.

Bistro in THE BARN

Set in idyllic countryside, Greenstead Family Barns Café is home to a café/restaurant with elegant bistro nights – making it one of Essex's hidden foodie hot spots.

At Greenstead Family Barns Café, everything revolves around the simple love of food. Owner Mark Grant took over the management of the 17th-century barn, which houses a popular café, in February 2017. He had been working as head chef at the café for quite some time, so when the owners decided to move on, Mark jumped at the chance to put his own stamp on the successful business.

Having spent a long time heading up the café kitchen – and boasting 25 years as a chef – there was no end to Mark's knowledge of the amazing local produce grown on site. He was adept transforming freshly grown new potatoes into delicious spring salads or pairing their home-grown apples with locally reared pork.

The thriving café offers hearty breakfasts featuring local sausages and free-range eggs, sandwiches, baguettes, ciabattas and jacket potatoes, alongside more substantial lunches. The options change to reflect the seasons and are crafted with care using ingredients from Greenstead Farm itself, as well as other neighbouring farms. A children's menu is also provided – assuming you can drag the little ones away from the soft play centre of course!

After the lunch-time rush, afternoon teas are the order of the day. Mouth-watering towers of sandwiches, scones and patisseries are made fresh on the premises and accompanied by a delightful selection of teas.

In June 2017, Mark launched the eagerly anticipated new bistro nights, which see the café reimagined as a cosy evening venue. He takes classic British and French dishes and gives them a bit of a modern twist, but the focus is always on letting the best Essex ingredients shine through in the cooking. The fully licenced nights take place on Friday and Saturday evenings and the menu changes every week.

From cosy coffees and cakes to elegant evening dining, Greenstead Family Barns has made the move from day-time favourite to stylish evening bistro, showcasing the plethora of exquisite produce grown in the area through creative yet classic cooking.

Greenstead Family Barns Café

PLEASE·ORDER·AT·COUNTER
BREAKFAST COFFEE SANDWICHES
LUNCH TEA JACKET·POTATO SALAD
AFTERNOON BAGUETTE

Todays Specials
BBQ pulled chicken - Sandwich·baguette
Coleslaw - or Jacket potato

Todays Soup
Roast vegetable

Homemade~Cakes
FRESH~
BREAD
CHILDREN
MENUS

Every Friday & Saturday Evening

Mark
GRANT'S
Bistro

Greenstead Family Barns Café

MARK GRANT'S DAUPHINOISE

I've chosen to share my dauphinoise potato recipe, because it has to be an ideal alternative to chips. There is very little cooking involved and little skill, but it has guaranteed impact with flavour and is fun to eat.

Preparation time: 15 minutes | Cooking time: 45 minutes | Serves 4

Ingredients

500g potatoes, peeled

1 litre double cream

4-6 cloves of garlic, peeled and kept whole (depending how strong you like garlic)

Optional extras:

Ham, chopped

Cheese, grated or crumbled

Cooked onions

Chives, chopped

Cream cheese

Puff pastry

Method

Preheat the oven to 160°c.

You can slice or dice your potatoes, it doesn't matter as long as they are cut to similar sizes.

Heat the cream with the garlic in a pan over a medium heat and bring to the boil. Don't let it boil over.

Place the potatoes in an ovenproof dish (or dishes if you want to make individual portions). If you are adding any optional extras, such as ham, cheese or cooked onions, mix these with the raw potatoes.

Pour the hot cream over the potatoes, allowing the garlic to sit on top of the potatoes.

Cover the dish with parchment paper and foil, place in the oven and cook for 45 minutes.

After cooking, mix some chives into some cream cheese and add to the Dauphinoise. Alternatively, add some grated cheddar or crumbled Stilton, or top with puff pastry to make a potato pie.

Burgers, Cocktails, PROPER.

Family-run Henry Burgers is inspired by the 'food and bar' culture of Europe and North America – and it has quickly won over the people of Essex with its laid-back charm.

Since it opened in October 2013, Henry Burgers has changed the face of the drinking and dining scene of Southend-on-Sea with its relaxed approach to eating and drinking. The business, which is owned by Henry and his mother Lisa, was so popular on opening that it had to move to a larger premises in Leigh-on-Sea after less than a year.

A family business through and through, Henry and Lisa remain the directors and only shareholders, and Henry's girlfriend is one of the front of house managers. With 18 years' experience in the hospitality industry, Henry was passionate about his new eatery idea from the start, which was inspired by his travels in North America and in Europe's vibrant cities.

When they moved into the two-storey space in 2014, they brought with them much of the ethos from their spiritual home in Southend, embodied in the unique upcycled features including the custom curved yew bar top. And of course, the focus remains on quality ingredients – from grass-fed British beef to small-batch spirits and British craft beers.

The beef is ground at a butcher 40 miles away, from a blend of chuck and rib cap. The hand-pressed patties contain nothing else, so can boast being gluten-free. The small menu also contains hand-cut sweet potato fries, which are made fresh each day. The regular fries are made from local, seasonal potatoes, and the buns are as fresh as can be. "They don't last as long as other bread buns," explains Henry, "but you can really taste the difference with no added preservatives and additives, not to mention the smell of fresh bread when they arrive!"

The family-friendly venue transforms after dark, especially at weekends, when the buzz increases and the guests (they don't have customers, only guests) kick back to enjoy the up-tempo vibes. Long-serving staff love to engage with guests, and Henry credits the amazing team for the vast number of regular visitors.

Now they are well and truly established, they are pushing themselves in myriad ways, from improving their impact on the environment and the community to developing an inspiring vegetarian and vegan menu. "The demand has been majorly increasing recently and we can only see it getting larger in future," says Henry, "plus, it's a fundamental part of our ethos – to serve the best meat and more veg!"

Henry Burgers
TEQUILA MOCKINGBIRD

Created by our sous chef Casey Savage, this burger started life as a special – it proved so popular it made it onto the main menu. The chicken needs to be marinated the night before.

Preparation time: 30 minutes, overnight marinating, and up to 2-4 hours proving
| Cooking time: 40 minutes | Serves 2

Ingredients

For the tequila and lime chicken:

2 skinless free-range chicken breast pieces

50ml 100% Blue Agave Tequila

50ml freshly squeezed lime juice

25ml freshly squeezed orange juice

½ tsp chilli powder

2 cloves garlic, minced

Drop of rapeseed oil

For the brioche buns:

125ml warm water

1 tsp dried yeast

1½ tbsp warm milk

1 tbsp caster sugar

225g strong/hard flour

½ tsp salt

2 tbsp unsalted butter

1 large egg, plus 1 egg, beaten, for glazing

For the cumin mayo:

100g mayonnaise

½ tsp ground cumin

To serve:

2-3 fresh jalapeños

2-3 red Birds Eye chillies

2 pineapple rings

Small pinch of caster sugar

⅛ iceberg lettuce, coarsely chopped

Salt

Rapeseed oil, for cooking

Method

For the tequila and lime chicken

Butterfly the chicken breasts. Mix the tequila, lime juice and orange juice in a dish. Add the chicken, chilli powder, minced garlic and a drop of rapeseed oil, and give it a good mix. Cover and place in the fridge overnight.

For the brioche buns

Mix the water, yeast, milk and sugar in a bowl, and let stand for 5 minutes. Put the flour and salt into a large mixing bowl, add the butter and mix with your fingertips until the mixture resembles breadcrumbs. Make a well in the centre of the buttery flour and add the yeast mixture and the egg. Use your hands to mix it into a sticky dough – if the mixture feels too wet at this stage, it will come together when kneading. Tip the dough out onto a floured work surface and knead for 10 minutes until soft and bouncy. It will still be sticky at first, but don't be tempted to add too much flour. Place in an oiled bowl, cover with cling film and set aside to rise for 1-3 hours or until doubled in size.

Once doubled in size, knock the air out and knead for 2 minutes. It won't be as sticky, but add flour if needed. Divide the dough in half. Roll into balls and arrange on a lined baking tray. Loosely cover with oiled cling film and leave for 1 hour or until doubled in size. Meanwhile, preheat the oven to 200°c/180°c fan/gas 6 and place a baking pan at the bottom.

Brush the buns with the beaten egg to glaze. Pour a cup of water into a baking tray and place at the bottom of the oven to create steam. Place the buns on a shelf above. Bake for 20 minutes or until golden, then let cool on a wire rack.

For the cumin mayo

Whisk together the mayonnaise and cumin in a small mixing bowl until smooth. Cover and place in the fridge until needed.

To cook and serve

Place the marinated chicken in a medium-hot frying pan with a drop of rapeseed oil. Add a small pinch of salt. Reduce the heat to medium and cook on each side for 8-10 minutes, until the juices run clear. Meanwhile, split the brioche buns and toast the insides under a medium grill. In a separate frying pan, fry the jalapeños and red chillies on a high heat for a couple of minutes until they start to brown. Fry the pineapple rings over high heat with a drop of rapeseed oil and a small pinch of caster sugar. On the bottom buns, apply the cumin mayo and shredded lettuce. Add a pineapple ring and cooked chicken breast to each. Top with the jalapeños and chillies. Add the tops of the buns and you are good to go.

Family PUBS

Marjoram Pubs, four modern British pubs in Essex, are keeping the independent pub spirit alive and well in their local communities.

Family-owned company Marjoram Pubs comprises of the Axe & Compasses, Aythorpe Roding; Angel & Harp, Great Dunmow; White Hart, Little Waltham; and Duke of York, Billericay. This independent business is owned by David and Sheila Hunt, along with their daughter Alessandra and son Joshua.

Having owned pubs around the Chelmsford area for 20 years, there isn't much David and Sheila don't know when it comes to running a great local. They are joined by daughter, Alessandra, and son, Joshua, who for 10 years worked in various London restaurants under some of the country's leading chefs.

The ethos of all four pubs centres around good value menus featuring homemade food. Food is served all day, with sections of the menu dedicated to fresh Billingsgate fish, pub classics, light lunches and chef's specials, among other fantastic dishes. Ingredients are hand-selected by David, who visits Billingsgate fish market, Spitalfields fruit and veg market and Smithfield meat market.

Accompanying the menu is a selection of lagers, wines, spirits and soft drinks, along with real ales with a rigorous guest policy featuring seasonal beers from small, regional and craft brewers on a regular basis.

What sets Marjoram Pubs apart from other venues is their 'multi-purpose' approach. Starting with breakfast served from 9am, the pubs offer food through lunch and dinner, along with teas, coffees and homemade cakes all day. Families are well catered for with a children's menu, colouring competitions, board games and even a selection of traditional penny sweets. Mid-week deals (2 for 1 on roasts, pub classics and fish dishes, for example) make it a good-value weeknight option too.

The family and management team have a clear vision for all their venues and are fighting to keep the independent pub alive as a community space – complete with touches you just don't get from a chain pub. Whether you are looking for a casual meeting with a friend, a three-course celebratory meal or merely a drink and a chat – everyone is warmly welcomed.

As all the pubs in the group are renowned for their fish dishes, it seemed only natural to provide one for this book. This dish was devised by sous chef at The Duke of York, Will Cummings, to whom the family would like to extend their thanks, in addition to the teams at all four pubs, GMs, head chefs and senior management team Laura, Martin and Nigel.

Marjoram Pubs
COD SUPREME WITH A CLAMS, PEA, BROAD BEANS AND SAMPHIRE BROTH

This dish was devised by sous chef at The Duke of York, Will Cummings, and is a great example of the fish dishes for which Marjoram Pubs have become renowned.

Preparation time: 20 minutes | Cooking time: 20 minutes | Serves 2

Ingredients

For the broth:

1 white onion, diced

3 cloves garlic, crushed

1 tsp olive oil

1 tsp salt

1 tsp black pepper

100ml white wine

200g clams, washed

100ml cream

200g samphire

2 salad tomatoes, de-seeded and diced

50g broad beans, peeled

50g peas

20g fresh parsley, finely chopped

20g fresh dill, finely chopped

For the cod:

2 cod supremes

Salt and black pepper

2 tsp rapeseed oil

Plain flour, to coat

Method

For the broth

Sweat the onion and garlic in a medium saucepan with the olive oil, salt and pepper. Add the white wine and clams to the saucepan, cover with a lid and cook on a high heat for roughly 3 minutes (until all the clams are open). Remove the lid and pour in the cream. When simmering, mix in the samphire, tomatoes, broad beans, peas, parsley and dill. Bring the broth back up to the boil, and simmer for a further 2 minutes.

For the cod

Preheat the oven to 180°c. Season the cod with salt and freshly ground black pepper. Lightly pat plain flour on the cod supremes on all sides. Heat the rapeseed oil in a non-stick frying pan to a medium-high heat. Place the pieces of cod skin-side down into the pan, applying gentle pressure to maintain the skin's contact with the pan.

After 1-2 minutes on each side of the supremes, place them onto an oven safe baking tray and bake in the oven for 6 minutes.

Serve the cod supremes with the broth.

Master MILLERS

One of the oldest businesses in Essex, Marriage's Millers is a fifth and sixth generation family business that has been supplying bakers with top-quality flour since 1824.

There are currently six members of the Marriage family running this long-standing business. Just as they were when they began business nearly 200 years ago, they are committed to selecting the best-quality wheat possible to create their famous flours. Today the range also includes organic varieties, seeded flours, and flours from ancient grains such as spelt and rye.

Luckily for Marriage's, Essex is one of the country's best wheat-growing areas. This means they can source much of their wheat from within a 30-mile radius of the mill, and from farming families who have been supplying Marriage's for generations.

They cater for a variety of customers on all sorts of scales, which means that the home baker can buy exactly the same quality flour as the professional bakery. Not only have their range of 18 home baking flours won a staggering 42 Great Taste Awards, they are also recommended by Paul Hollywood and Hugh Fearnley-Whittingstall in their cookbooks.

The success of Marriage's comes down to the commitment to quality, and they achieve this by choosing the very best wheat. For bread flours, they source some high-protein wheat from Canada to supplement the local Essex grains. They maintain a fine balance between the traditional technique of stone-milling and the modern process of roller-milling – using each technique for specific types of flour.

Marriage's stoneground wholemeal flours are milled on horizontal French Burr stones that are over a hundred years old. The resulting flavour is deep and nutty, and the flour is wholesome and nutritious.

Stocked in a plethora of local delis, farm shops, health food stores and the East of England Co-op, Marriage's flour is also available online through Ocado, Abel and Cole, and their own website. It is important to everyone at Marriage's that home bakers can access these high-quality flours easily – if people take the time to bake, they want to be able to guarantee good end results, so it is worth using the very best quality ingredients to ensure success.

With the consistent results of Marriage's flours (and a little practice!), bakers can aim to achieve the same excellent results as the independent artisan bakeries across East Anglia and beyond who use Marriage's flour to produce the finest breads, cakes, pastry, pasta and pizza.

Marriage's Millers
FOCACCIA

A rustic bread from Italy, this focaccia is flavoured with fresh rosemary, thyme and parsley, plus olive oil and sea salt, then baked in a rectangular roasting tin. Eat with dips, olives and salami. The next day, cut the bread into thick slices and grill to make bruschetta.

Preparation time: 2 hours, including resting time | Cooking time: 25 minutes | Makes 1

Ingredients

For the dough:

500g Marriage's Finest Strong White flour

2 tsp sea salt

2 tbsp chopped fresh herbs (a mix of rosemary, thyme, parsley or sage)

7g dried fast-action yeast or 14g fresh yeast

3 tbsp olive oil

300ml tepid water

To finish:

A few sprigs of fresh rosemary

3 tbsp olive oil

1 tsp sea salt

Method

For the dough

Lightly grease a large roasting tin (about 25 x 35cm).

Mix the flour, salt, herbs and yeast in a mixing bowl. Make a well in the centre and pour in the olive oil and water. Tip the dough onto a table and knead for 8-10 minutes. A mixer can also be used.

Place the dough back into the bowl and cover with oiled cling film or a damp tea towel. Rest in a warm place until the dough has doubled in size. This will take approximately an hour.

Tip the dough into the greased roasting tin. Knock the dough down, so it is evenly flat and covers the base of the roasting tin. Cover with oiled cling film as before and leave to rest for 40-50 minutes.

To finish

Dimple the dough by firmly pressing your fingertips into the dough. Push small sprigs of rosemary into the dimples, then cover and rest for another 15 minutes. Meanwhile, preheat the oven 220°c (425°f/Gas 7). Drizzle the olive oil over the risen dough and sprinkle with the salt, then bake for 20-25 minutes until golden brown. Turn out onto a wire rack. Best eaten warm.

MARRIAGE'S
THE MASTER MILLERS
FINEST
FLOUR
SUITABLE FOR BREAD MACHINES
HIGH PROTEIN FOR BREAD, ROLLS, PIZZA BASES & PUFF PASTRY

Please ask a
member of staff if
you would like your
bread sliced

The beauty of
BREAD

Set within a Victorian dairy farm on the Essex-Hertfordshire border, Mayfield Farm Bakery is an idyllic spot to learn the art of baking hand-crafted bread.

Since it was established in 2010, Mayfield Farm Bakery has become one of Essex's favourite makers of artisan bread. Thanks to its discerning choice of suppliers, the bread hand-crafted at Mayfield Farm Bakery has gained a myriad of fans, featured on television more than once and chalked up a number of awards – including the coveted World Bread Awards.

They use organic flour from W H Marriage (another local Essex business, these millers have a reputation that is second to none) and where possible, they use many other local products from Essex, including Thursday Cottage jams and chutneys and Duchess Oils from Sheering.

The beautiful setting amongst the rural landscape provides the ideal backdrop for the bakery, as well as the farm shop and tea room. The building has been tastefully restored, celebrating its history while being light, bright and modern inside.

On entering, visitors are greeted with the mouth-watering array of breads and cakes on display – and, if you are early enough, you can even see the bakers working away! Passing through to the farm shop takes you past a great selection of jams and honeys, and for those who like to make bread, a great range of flours.

The farm shop itself contains a beautiful selection of patisserie, both individual portions as well as whole tarts, bavarois and pies to serve at home. The take away section offers hot food and drinks as well as sandwiches and salads. So popular are these, that customers have been known to travel from far and wide to sample them – including cyclists who have peddled from London to tuck into a fresh sausage roll! Chutneys, dipping oils, cheeses, antipasti and stylish kitchenware complete the selection.

On sunny days, customers can enjoy breakfast, lunch or afternoon tea al fresco on the courtyard. The perfect spot to enjoy the stunning scenery while tucking into sandwiches using our speciality bread, dainty hand-made patisseries and, of course, delicious homemade scones topped with cream and jam.

With renovated access for those with disabilities and plenty of parking available, Mayfield Farm Bakery has made sure that absolutely everyone can come and enjoy the special artisan bread, hand-crafted patisseries and lovingly home-cooked food.

Mayfield Farm Bakery

GLUTEN-FREE BROWNIES WITH RASPBERRIES

Dense, rich and luxurious, these gluten-free brownies pop with the vibrant flavour of raspberries.

Preparation time: 15 minutes | Cooking time: 45 minutes | Serves 24

Ingredients

200g quality plain chocolate

250g butter

A few drops of vanilla essence

4 medium eggs

300g caster sugar

125g gluten-free flour (we use Dove's)

100g frozen raspberries

Icing sugar, for dusting

Method

Preheat the oven to 190°c. Melt the chocolate and butter in a bowl over a pan of hot water, add the vanilla essence and lightly beat in the eggs. Add the sugar and flour to the bowl, and combine all the ingredients. Stir in the frozen raspberries gently.

Line a brownie tin with baking parchment approximately 28 x 18cm.

Spoon in the mixture and level the top carefully. Bake in the centre of the preheated oven for 40-45 minutes until set to the touch in the centre – it should spring back slightly.

Take out of the oven and leave to cool a little, then turn out carefully onto a wire rack to cool completely. Cut into approximately 24 squares, depending on your preferred portion size, and dust with sifted icing sugar.

Mayfield Farm Bakery
LAVENDER CAKE

A subtle floral flavour of lavender is infused into the cake mixture of this light cake, topped with a luscious buttercream.

Preparation time: 30 minutes, plus 30 minutes infusing | Cooking time: 40 minutes | Serves 8-10

Ingredients

For the cake:

480ml whole milk

6 sprigs of lavender flowers

440g unsalted butter

600g caster sugar

6 eggs

600g self-raising flour

For the buttercream:

200g unsalted butter

400g icing sugar, sifted

2 tsp vanilla essence

Honey to taste, optional

For the decoration:

Edible lavender flowers

Method

For the cake

Preheat the oven to 180°c. Line two 10-inch cake tins with baking parchment.

Place the milk in a saucepan and bring to simmering point, then add the lavender flowers and set aside for 30 minutes.

Cream the butter and sugar until light and fluffy, and then add the eggs, one at a time. If the mixture starts to split, add a spoonful of the flour. Once all the eggs have been added, sift in the flour and fold carefully into the mixture using a metal spoon.

Strain the milk (to remove all the flowers) into a jug, and check you still have 480ml; if not, top up with cold milk. Gently mix the milk into the cake mixture until combined.

Spoon the mixture into the prepared cake tins to about half full. Place in the preheated oven for 40 minutes until baked. Pierce the centre with a metal skewer; if it comes out clean, the cake is ready.

Allow the cakes to cool for 10-15 minutes in the tins, and then remove them from the tins and leave to cool on a cooling rack.

For the buttercream

To make the buttercream, beat the softened butter in a large bowl until soft, pale and fluffy. Add the icing sugar and beat until all the sugar is incorporated. Flavour with vanilla essence and honey, if using. Once the cake is completely cold, use one-third to fill the centre of the cake and the remainder for the top. Decorate with lavender flowers.

Mayfield Farm Bakery

RED PEPPER AND ASPARAGUS QUICHE

This is a savoury staple in our tea room.

Preparation time: 30 minutes, plus 90 minutes resting | Cooking time: 1 hour | Serves 8-10

Ingredients

For the shortcrust pastry:

175g plain flour, plus extra for dusting

Pinch of salt

75g butter

For the filling:

150g mature Cheddar, grated

100g red Leicester, grated

1 red pepper

75g butter

1 small bunch of asparagus, woody ends snapped off

200ml double cream

100ml milk

5 eggs

Salt and pepper, to taste

Method

For the shortcrust pastry

Sift the plain flour into a bowl with a pinch of salt. Rub in the butter until the butter and flour resembles fine breadcrumbs. Add sufficient cold water a tablespoon at a time to combine into a firm dough. Wrap in cling film and chill in the fridge for 1 hour.

Roll out the pastry on a lightly floured surface, fold over a rolling pin and place over a well-buttered flan ring. Gently push the pastry into the corners. Allow to rest again for 30 minutes. Prick the bottom with a fork.

Preheat the oven to 190°c. Line the pastry base with greaseproof paper and fill with baking beans or rice. Place on a baking tray and bake for 20 minutes. Lift out the greaseproof paper and baking beans or rice, and put the pastry case back in the oven for a further 5 minutes. Allow to cool.

For the filling

Sprinkle the cheeses in the pastry case, finely slice the red pepper and arrange on the cheese so the peppers radiate out from the centre. Between each of the pepper slices, place a stem of asparagus.

Combine the cream, milk and eggs in a jug, season well with salt and pepper, and gently pour over the asparagus and peppers.

Bake for 30-40 minutes until set. Remove from the oven and allow to cool. Can be served hot or cold.

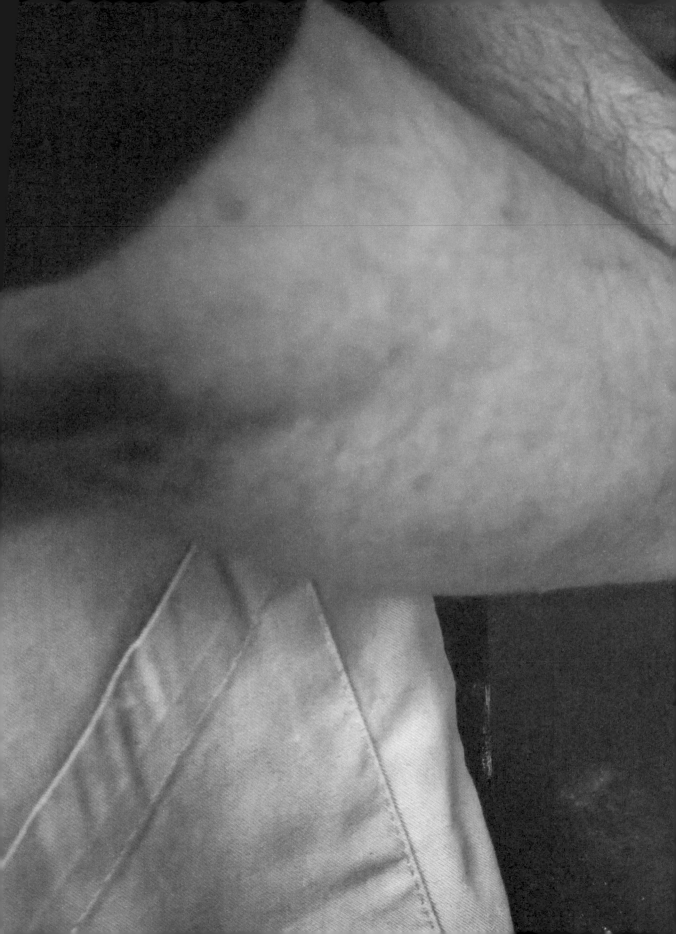

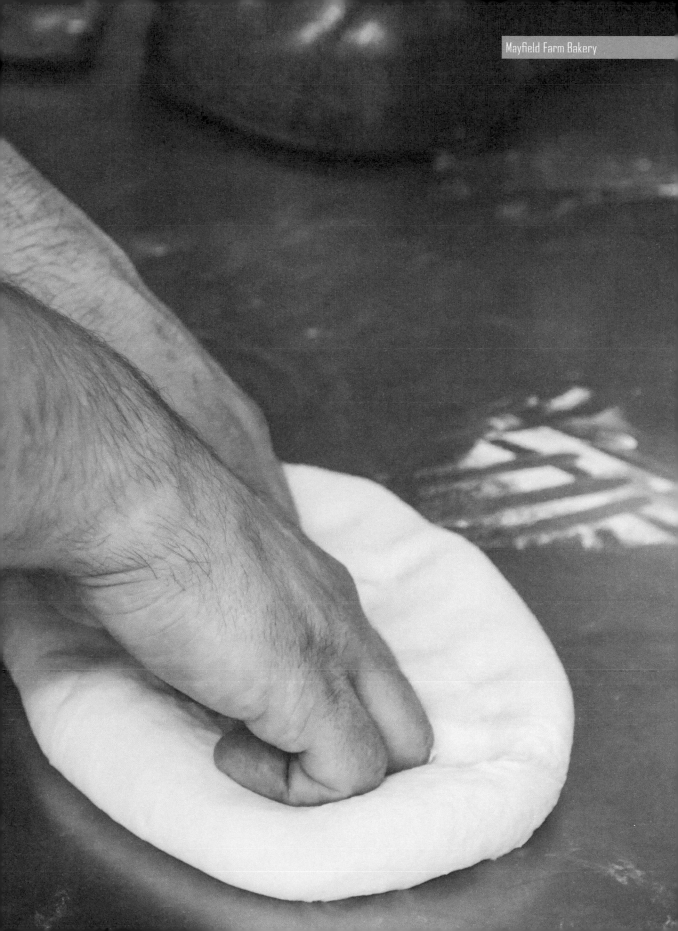

Mayfield Farm Bakery
STILTON & RAISIN BREAD

This is a bread we often teach at our Bakery School, as it really shows what you can do with a good white dough to make a delicious speciality bread – ideal served with summer salads, on its own, or with soup.

Preparation time: 30 minutes, plus 90 minutes proving | Cooking time: 20 minutes | Makes 2 loaves

Ingredients

600g WH Marriage's strong white flour, plus extra for dusting

10g cooking salt

12g vegetable shortening

15g fresh baker's yeast

350g water

250g Stilton, or to taste

150g California raisins, or to taste

50g semolina, for sprinkling

Method

Weigh out the flour then place it into a mixing bowl, add the salt to one side of the bowl, and the yeast to the otherside of the flour, keeping the salt well away from the yeast. Add the vegetable shortening and water, gradually incorporating the flour until the mixture forms a smooth, firm dough.

Turn out the dough on to a floured surface and knead well for approximately 10 minutes until smooth and elastic. To knead the dough, stretch the dough with the heel of your hand forward, then bring the front edge back with your fingers, and repeat. If you have a mixer with a dough hook, you can use the mixer for about 6-7 minutes. Cover with a plastic bowl or tea towel, leave to prove for 45 minutes. Once it is ready it will feel springy to the touch.

Divide the dough into two, mould each into a ball, cover and leave for 20 minutes.

Flatten out each ball with your hands until it is about 15mm thick in a round shape. Sprinkle 75g of Stilton and 75g (or to taste) of California raisins on each dough. Roll the dough up like a Swiss roll and work into a cigar shape with the join at the bottom, then seal carefully with your fingers.

Cover and leave to prove for 20 minutes until doubled in size.

Preheat the oven to 220°c. Place an empty metal roasting dish in the bottom of the oven.

Once the doughs have been proved, sprinkle the tops of the loaves with semolina and dust lightly with flour. Slash the top of each loaf from end to end with a sharp knife. Place about 50g of crumbled Stilton in the slash for decoration. Place on a baking sheet lined with baking paper.

Put the bread in the oven, tip half a cup of cold water into the bottom of the roasting dish and shut the door to create steam. Bake for 17-20 minutes or until golden.

Allow to cool and enjoy!

Mayfield Farm Bakery
TARTE AU CITRON

A firm favourite with our customers in the farm shop to serve at home, and to eat in the tea room for pudding. Delicious served with cream!

Preparation time: 30 minutes, plus 2 hours chilling and 12 hours setting | Cooking time: 30 minutes | Serves 4

Ingredients

For the sweet pastry:

125g butter, chilled

125g icing sugar

A few drops of vanilla essence (to taste)

1 medium egg

250g plain flour

For the lemon filling:

Zest of 1 lemon

75ml lemon juice

100g granulated sugar

2 medium eggs

125g unsalted butter, cubed

For the decoration:

Whipped cream

Fresh fruit

Method

For the sweet pastry

Cut the chilled butter into small cubes and beat until soft. Add the icing sugar and vanilla essence and combine well. Add the egg and flour, and mix until the pastry comes together to form a ball. Wrap in cling film and allow to rest in the fridge for 1-2 hours until well chilled. The pastry can be made a day in advance.

Roll the chilled pastry into a round large enough to line your pastry case. Fold the pastry over a rolling pin and lift over the flan ring. Press the pastry into the corners, prick the bottom of the case, line with greaseproof paper and fill with rice or baking beans. Chill for 30 minutes. Meanwhile, preheat the oven to 190°c.

Bake the pastry base in the preheated oven for about 20 minutes, depending on the thickness of the pastry. Carefully lift out the greaseproof paper and baking beans or rice, and continue to cook for a further 5 minutes until golden in colour.

For the lemon filling

Use the finest zester on a box grater, remove the zest from the lemon; you will have about a teaspoonful. Set aside. Squeeze the lemon juice through a sieve into a saucepan to remove any pips and fleshy pieces of lemon. Add the zest and sugar. Break the eggs into a cup and mix with a fork. Tip into the saucepan. Whisk all the ingredients with a hand whisk or small electric whisk together off the heat.

Place on a gentle heat, stir continually until the mixture becomes smooth and thick. It will become lumpy if left or overcooked. Remove from the hob.

Add the cubed pieces of butter a few at a time, and whisk gently to incorporate. Pour into the tart shell and allow to set for 12 hours.

For the decoration

Decorate to taste with cream rosettes and fresh fruit.

Radio Essex
BRILLIANT BREAKFAST
MINI OMMIES

This recipe is brought to you from Radio Essex's Hit Music Breakfast with Chris and Abbie. These mini omelettes are delicious served hot or cold. Add to a salad to make a meal or eat them on their own for a healthy snack.

Preparation time: 10 minutes | Cooking time: 20 minutes | Serves 12

Ingredients

6 eggs

Handful of spinach, torn

25g feta cheese, crumbled

12 cherry tomatoes, quartered

Black pepper

Method

Preheat the oven to 180°c. Lightly whisk the eggs in a bowl. Add a sprinkle of pepper, according to taste.

In a separate bowl, add the torn spinach, crumbled feta and the quartered cherry tomatoes. Divide the contents equally between the 12 holes of a cupcake or muffin tray. Pour the egg mixture into the 12 moulds, coating all the ingredients.

Bake in the preheated oven for 20 minutes.

That's it! Easy peasy and a great way to start your day! With lots of protein to kick-start your metabolism and keep you full for longer, they're a perfect hit for breakfast!

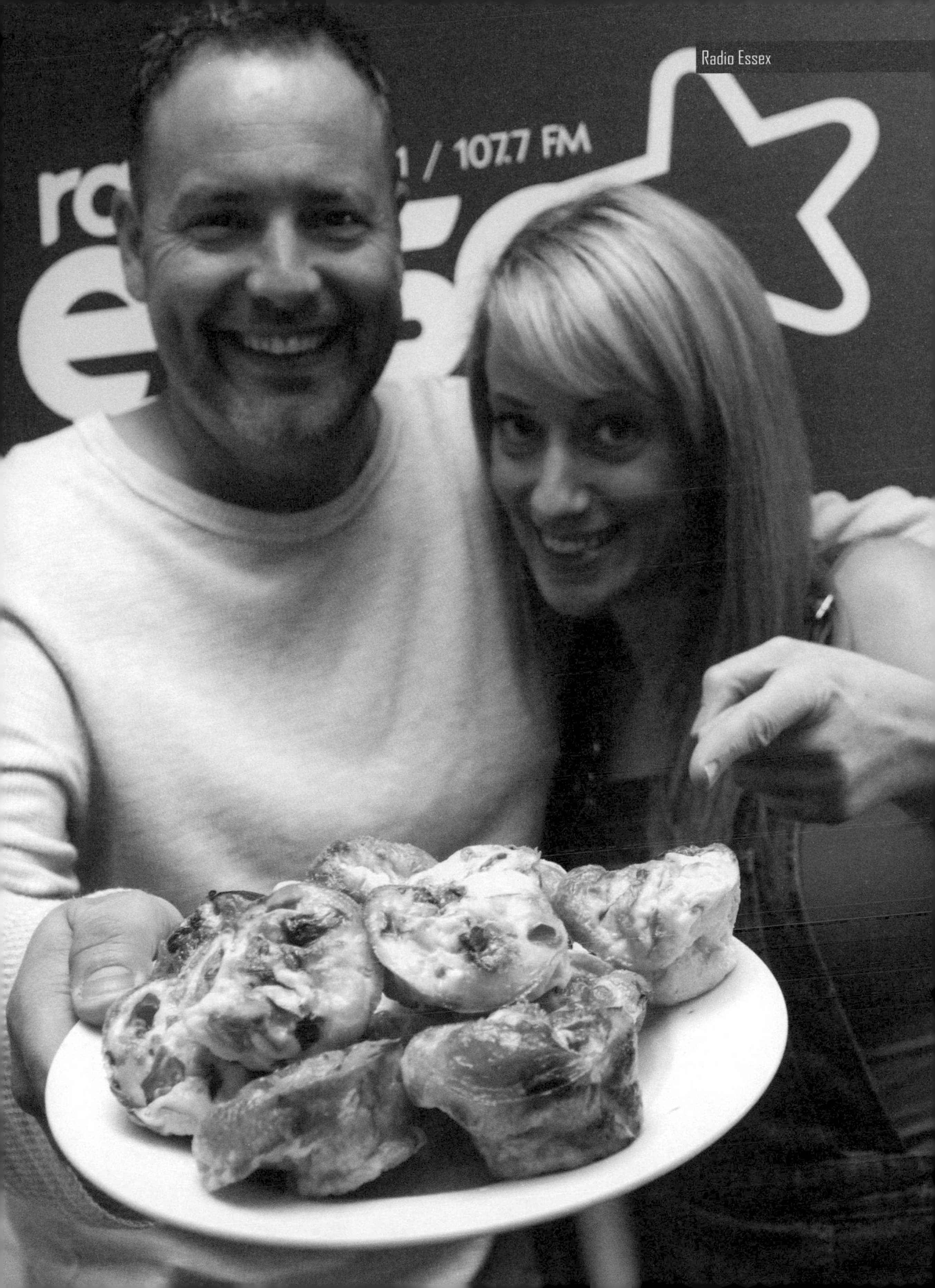

Radio Essex

The Red Cow
OPEN BEEF WELLINGTON

A postcard-worthy pub, complete with thatched roof and rural charm, The Red Cow is an idyllic countryside escape serving fresh, locally sourced food in cosy surroundings. Owned and managed by Toby Didier'Serre and his partner Alexis Beeching, The Red Cow is the embodiment of Toby and Alexis's love for good food, great drinks and convivial hospitality. Before moving to The Red Cow in 2010, Toby had gained a reputation for excellence as head chef at Goose Fat and Garlic in Sawbridgeworth and Chequers in Matching Green, where his passion for local produce saw the pub receive much acclaim.

Thanks to its stunning countryside location, The Red Cow is popular with walkers and shooting parties – well-behaved dogs are welcome in the bar area, too. From hearty breakfasts and sustaining lunches to relaxed evening dining, this is a pub that celebrates its setting, its community and its many regular customers. This is one of their signature dishes, which is finished in The Red Cow with a cream and whisky mushroom sauce and served with sautéed potatoes.

Preparation time: 20 minutes | Cooking time: 30 minutes | Serves 1

Ingredients

170-200g beef fillet

½ tbsp tomato purée

½ tbsp cranberry sauce

Splash of white wine vinegar

Pinch of cayenne pepper

½ lime

115g puff pastry

4 cherry tomatoes, halved

Salt and pepper

To serve:

Sautéed potatoes

Cream whisky mushroom sauce

Green beans or peas

Watercress, to garnish

Method

Cook the fillet in a hot dry griddle pan to mark the steak with a criss-cross effect on both sides. I would recommend cooking it medium-rare. Do not use oil as you want the fillet nice and dry. Cook the fillet for about 5 minutes, to your liking, then leave on a baking tray to rest for 5 minutes in a warm place.

For the cranberry and tomato salsa, place the tomato purée, cranberry sauce, white wine vinegar, cayenne pepper and salt to taste in a small pan. Simmer for a few minutes, then allow to cool. Squeeze in the lime and mix well.

Preheat the oven to 180°c. Roll out puff pastry to 6mm thick and cut out a 12.5cm circle. Chill, then bake for 15 minutes. Allow to cool.

To serve

Place the sautéed potatoes in the centre of a bistro dish, and put the fillet on top with the puff pastry crouton, top with the salsa and halved cherry tomatoes. Spoon the sauce around the outside, add greens and garnish with watercress.

The Red Cow

Seaside SPECIALTIES

Holding a special place in the hearts of the locals in Leigh-on-Sea,
The Sand Bar and Seafood Co. has been delighting Essex's diners since 1998.

A family business through and through, The Sand Bar and Seafood Co. was opened by Ann Donnelly in August 1998 – and 19 years later, there are countless members of the family involved in the running of this Leigh-on-Sea local gem.

It is not only the blood relatives who are treated like family here, some of the customers have been frequenting the bar and restaurant for 19 years. "We have watched customers' babies turn into adults and become customers themselves," says Louise, Ann's daughter. "It is such a pleasure to be a fixture in the lives of many local people."

The atmosphere of The Sand Bar and Seafood Co. is inspired by the family's love of relaxed European dining. Louise describes herself as a huge Francophile and dog-lover, and has spent many holidays being welcomed along with her dogs into friendly bars in France. She wanted to recreate this relaxed ambience, so well-behaved pooches are welcome in the bar area. The upstairs restaurant remains dog-free, but guests can order snacks and light bites in the bustling bar.

The home-from-home feeling continues upstairs in the more formal setting of the restaurant. White linen tablecloths provide the perfect stage for head chef Grae Walker's dishes to take centre stage. The menu changes three times a week according to what fresh produce they get from Billingsgate Fish Market each day. Think marinated herring, oysters, or soft-shell crab to start, followed by Sand Bar bouillabaisse, clam linguine, sea bass fillet or even a generous whole lobster tail thermidor for the main course.

Louise is a member of PETA and the whole family passionately support 'meat-free Monday' by offering two veggie courses and a scoop of ice cream for £9.99. They do their best to accommodate vegetarians and vegans on all days, of course, with options like linguine in tomato and crushed olive sugo or vegan jambalaya.

An extensive drinks list and selection of homemade desserts and ice creams completes the meal. It has always been really important to the family to keep their prices as fair as possible, and they work hard to keep their margins to a minimum to ensure The Sand Bar and Seafood Co. remains one of Leigh-on-Sea's most friendly and welcoming venues.

The Sand Bar and Seafood Co.

The Sand Bar & Seafood Co.
'AFTER EIGHTEEN' ICE CREAM

Quick and simple, and great for someone having a dinner party
with little time to prepare. You will need a mixer with a whisk attachment, a
measuring jug, plastic Tupperware (with a lid) and a spatula – for licking!

Preparation time: 20 minutes, plus 5-6 hours freezing | Makes 25-30 scoops

Ingredients

1 box After Eight mints

397g tin condensed milk

600ml whipping cream

100–150ml crème de menthe
(depending on your taste buds)

Method

Break up the After Eight mints, place them in a bowl and set aside.

In a mixing bowl, place the condensed milk. Add the whipping cream and whisk slowly. Gradually build up the speed as the mixture whips up. When you get a full whipped cream effect, add the crème de menthe and slowly whisk that through until the creamy mixture is a light green colour throughout.

Start to layer your Tupperware, first with a generous layer of crème de menthe cream mixture, then a generous amount of crumbled chocolate mints. Keep repeating the process until you have run out of mixture and chocolate mints. Put the lid on tightly.

Place in the freezer for at least 5-6 hours and you are good to go. Enjoy.

The Saracens Head Hotel
SPRING SAFFRON RISOTTO

In the middle of historic Great Dunmow lies a beautiful Grade II listed 15th-century coaching inn, which is home to The Saracens Head Hotel. This characterful building has been lovingly and tastefully refurbished, from its 30 luxurious bedrooms to its popular restaurant. The restaurant has become a favourite dining destination for locals, who have been won over by head chef Guy Segev's creative approach to modern British and European dining.
The kitchen makes the most of the plethora of local produce available in the surrounding countryside, from fruit and vegetables to meat and fish, which means the menu changes regularly as a reflection of the seasons. An extensive drinks list sets this restaurant apart, thanks to a carefully chosen selection of wines from around the world and an impressive gin bar – which contains a whopping 50 varieties!
This is a beautiful spring dish by head chef Guy Segev, whose training at a top Italian restaurant in Harrogate influenced his love of modern European dishes.

Preparation time: 10 minutes | Cooking time: 40 minutes | Serves 4

Ingredients

1 litre vegetable stock

¼ tsp crumbled saffron

20ml olive oil

15g butter

50g shallots, diced

1 garlic clove

350g Arborio risotto rice

100ml white wine

100g stem broccoli, diced and blanched

100g green beans, diced and blanched

100g peas

50g baby spinach, finely shredded

10g flat leaf parsley, chopped

30g goat's cheese, grated

Salt and pepper

Pea shoots and edible flowers, to garnish

Method

Heat the stock and saffron in a saucepan. In a separate pan, heat the oil and half the butter over a low heat, add the shallots and garlic, and fry gently for about 15 minutes, or until softened but not coloured.

Add the rice and turn up the heat – the rice will now begin to lightly fry, so keep stirring it. After 1 minute, it will look slightly translucent. Add the wine and keep stirring. Any harsh alcohol flavours will evaporate and leave the rice with just a tasty essence.

Once the wine has cooked into the rice, add a ladleful of hot stock and a good pinch of salt and pepper. Turn the heat down to a simmer so the rice doesn't cook too quickly on the outside. Keep adding ladlefuls of stock, stirring and almost massaging the creamy starch out of the rice, allowing each ladleful to be absorbed before adding the next. This will take around 10 minutes.

Taste the rice — is it cooked? Carry on adding stock until the rice is soft but with a slight bite. Don't forget to check the seasoning carefully. If you run out of stock before the rice is cooked, add some boiling water. Add the broccoli, green beans and peas, and cook for 2-3 minutes, then add the spinach, parsley and goat's cheese. Remove the saucepan from the heat; add the remaining butter and stir well. Garnish with pea shoots and edible flowers.

New World WINE

Family-run vineyard, West Street Vineyard, has been open only four years, and has already won a Cellar Door award thanks to its passionate approach to Essex wine.

West Street Vineyard was bought by the Mohan family in 2009. For Jane and Stephen, it was a long-awaited chance to put their dream of owning a vineyard into action. They had both worked on vineyards in Europe when they were younger, and the joy of winemaking had remained with them. Jane remembers being sent to France, aged 17, to learn French. She spent many happy months living on a vineyard (and developing a love of rosé wine!).

"Vineyards tend to be in some of the world's most beautiful landscapes," enthuses Jane, "but for me, it's also about the culture that surrounds wine in these places – people getting together to enjoy great food, great wine and great company."

Essex may seem very far from the great wine regions of Italy and France, but the county holds much beauty of its own. Jane is passionate about the fantastic local produce in her home county, not to mention the stunning scenery. The six-acre plot in Coggeshall was the perfect spot for the Mohans to bring the Languedoc to Essex.

"Making wine is always about making the best possible wine you can from the land you are on," explains Jane. And this approach to getting the very best from the land extends to the food on offer at West Street Vineyard too. It was important to them to create a lovely place to eat, which would serve home-cooked food made with local ingredients. In the restaurant, they make everything in house – right down to the tomato ketchup!

For Jane, everything they do comes down to hospitality. It's a very personal place, a place the family have put their heart into, so they are passionate about sharing it with people and welcoming them to the vineyard as if it were their home. This simple philosophy runs through everything they do, including the wine school, which runs introduction to wine courses, as well as vineyard walks and tastings.

Viticulture may be one of the oldest forms of agriculture, but it is only recently making waves in the UK. With enthusiastic viticulturists like the Mohan family exploring the potential for creating award-winning wines in the idyllic English countryside, it is an exciting time to be involved in the industry.

West Street Vineyard
BEEF CHEEKS WITH MEDITERRANEAN VEGETABLES AND TOMATO COULIS

A warming dish that marries good-quality red wine with beef cheeks and slow-cooking to achieve tender perfection. A medley of roasted vegetables and a flavoursome tomato coulis finishes the dish off beautifully.

Preparation time: 30 minutes | Cooking time: 4 hours | Serves 4

Ingredients

For the beef cheeks:

4 beef cheeks (125-175g per portion)

1 large white onion

2 carrots

2 celery sticks

3-4 sprigs thyme

Red wine, to cover

For the vegetables:

1 red and 1 yellow pepper, chopped

1 aubergine, chopped

1 large red onion, roughly chopped

12-16 cherry tomatoes, on the vine

1 garlic bulb, halved

5 large potatoes, diced

2 sprigs thyme

Large handful of rosemary

Salt and pepper

Good-quality olive oil, for drizzling

For the tomato coulis:

1 small red onion, diced

400g can of tomatoes

1 tsp honey

2 tsp sugar

2 tsp good-quality balsamic vinegar

Method

For the beef cheeks

Preheat the oven to 160°c. Trim the fat from the beef cheek or ask your butcher to do it for you. Seal the beef cheek in a hot pan until it has browned in colour.

Roughly chop the onion, carrots and celery then layer in an ovenproof dish with the sprigs of thyme. Place the beef on top of the vegetables and cover with the wine. Cover with greaseproof paper and a layer of tin foil. Cook in the preheated oven for around 4 hours until the beef is tender.

For the vegetables

While the beef is cooking place the peppers, aubergines, onions, cherry vine tomatoes, halved garlic bulb and diced potatoes in an oven tray. Drizzle with good-quality olive oil and scatter over the fresh herbs. Season well and roast in the oven at 180°c for 35-40 minutes.

For the tomato coulis

Place the diced onion in a food processor with the tomatoes and blitz to a fine paste. Transfer to a saucepan, add the remaining ingredients and heat gently. Season with salt and pepper to taste.

To serve

Once the beef is tender, leave to rest. Pour the coulis on to each plate for serving. Arrange the roasted vegetables so each person receives a generous portion and then place the rested beef cheek on the vegetables. Serve immediately.

The
DIRECTORY

These great businesses have supported the making of this book;
please support and enjoy them.

The Anchor Riverside
284 Ferry Road
Hockley SS5 6ND
Telephone: 01702 230 205
Website:
www.theanchorhullbridge.co.uk
*Pub and restaurant enjoying a superb
waterfront position and serving a wide
range of innovative dishes.*

Boadicea Bar & Restaurant
Haven Road
Colchester
Essex CO2 8FU
Telephone: 01206 862 822
Website: www.boadiceacol.com
*Classic British dishes with a modern
twist, in a rustic and industrial yet
modern environment.*

Deersbrook Farm
Littles Lane
Shalford Green
Braintree
Essex CM7 5AZ
Telephone: 01371 850671
or 07766 543493
Website: www.deersbrookfarm.com
*Family-run farm in the beautiful Essex
countryside producing high-quality
native, pasture-fed beef.*

Duchess Oil
New House Farm
Sheering Lower Road
Sawbridgeworth
Hertfordshire CM21 9LE
Telephone: 01279 726741
Website: www.duchessoil.co.uk
*Extra-virgin rapeseed oil that's grown,
pressed and bottled on a farm on the
border of Hertfordshire and Essex.*

The Eight Bells
18 Bridge Street
Saffron Walden
Essex CB10 1BU
Telephone: 01799 522790
Website: www.8bells-pub.co.uk
*The Eight Bells is a much-loved local in
the heart of Saffron Walden serving classic
pub food and creative seasonal specials.*

Great Clerkes Farm
Little Sampford
Saffron Walden
Essex CB10 2QJ
Telephone: 07968148896 /
07801132334
Website:
www.greatclerkesfarmfoods.co.uk
Purveyors of the finest free-range poultry.

Great Garnetts
Bishops Green
Barnston, Nr Dunmow
Essex CM6 1NE
Telephone: 01245 231 331
Website: www.greatgarnetts.co.uk
*Naturally reared and totally traceable
pork and turkey.*

Greenstead Family Barns Café
Greenstead Green, nr Halstead
Essex CO9 1QY
Telephone: 01787 472807
Website:
www.greensteadfamilybarnscafe.co.uk
*Located in the idyllic Essex countryside,
this 17th-century barn houses a cosy café/
restaurant.*

Henry Burgers
141 Broadway
Leigh-on-Sea
Essex SS9 1PJ
Telephone: 01702 715390
Website: www.henryburgers.co.uk
*Delicious burgers... outstanding cocktails...
party vibes.*

Marjoram Pubs

The Axe & Compasses
Dunmow Road
Aythorpe Roding
Essex CM6 1PP
Telephone: 01279 876 648
Website:
www.theaxeandcompasses.co.uk
*A fantastic local pub and restaurant in
the beautiful village of Aythorpe Roding,
close to Chelmsford, Great Dunmow and
Stansted Airport, serving an array of cask
ales, great wines and delicious, freshly
cooked food.*

The Angel & Harp
Church Street
Great Dunmow
Essex CM6 2AD
Telephone: 01371 859 259
Website: www.angelandharp.co.uk
*Located in the historic market town of
Great Dunmow, a stone's throw away
from Stansted Airport, this Grade
II-listed building was substantially
refurbished to provide a stylish yet relaxed
pub environment and beer garden suitable
for everyone.*

The White Hart
The Street
Little Waltham
Essex CM3 3NY
Telephone: 01245 360 205
Website www.whitehartessex.co.uk
*Local pub in the beautiful village of Little
Waltham, close to Chelmsford town centre,
serving an array of cask ales, great wines
and delicious, freshly cooked food.*

Duke of York
Southend Road
Billericay
Essex CM11 2PR
Telephone: 01277 887 581
Website: www.dukeofyorkessex.co.uk
*Located in Billericay, The Duke of York
holds weekly offers, the best Sunday roasts,
children's menu, food theme events, beer
festivals and more making it the ideal
family local.*

W & H Marriage & Sons Limited
Chelmer Mills
New Street
Chelmsford
Essex CM1 1PN
Telephone: 01245 354455
Website: www.flour.co.uk
*Milling flour in Essex since 1824, W &
H Marriage & Sons Ltd are committed to
selecting the best-quality wheat, sourcing
much from farmers based within 25–30
miles of Chelmer Mills in Chelmsford.*

Mayfield Farm Bakery & School
Sheering Road
Old Harlow
Essex CM17 0JP
Telephone: 01279 411774
Website:
www.mayfieldfarmbakery.co.uk
*World Bread Award-winning artisan
bakery making speciality breads and
patisserie, with an on-site tea room and
farm shop.*

Pastry Development Limited
Thomas Leatherbarrow
Telephone: 07930453852
Website:
www.pastrydevelopement.co.uk
*Specialist in bespoke desserts and luxury
chocolates – as one of the leaders in
hospitality and concept design consultancy,
you are assured of excellence throughout all
services offered.*

The Red Cow
11 High Street
Chrishall
Royston SG8 8RN
Telephone: 01763 838792
Website: www.theredcow.com
*Beautiful pub guaranteeing a friendly
welcome in beautiful surroundings and
delicious, homemade dishes.*

The Sand Bar & Seafood Co. Ltd
71 Broadway
Leigh-on-sea
Essex SS9 1PE
Telephone: 01702 480 067
Website:
www.sandbarandseafood.co.uk
*A family-run establishment specialising in
fish and seafood, with a strong vegetarian
and vegan section on the menu.*

The Saracens Head Hotel
High Street
Great Dunmow
Essex CM6 1AG
Telephone: 01371 873901
Website:
www.saracenshead-hotel.co.uk
*Grade II-listed hotel and restaurant in the
middle of the beautiful Essex countryside
serving seasonal food prepared using fresh
and local ingredients.*

**The West Street Vineyard &
Restaurant**
West Street
Coggeshall
Essex CO6 1NS
Telephone: 01376 563303
Website: www.weststreetvineyard.co.uk
*Vineyard producing award-winning
wine with on-site wine school and
restaurant.*

Other titles in the 'Get Stuck In' series

The Brighton & Sussex Cook Book features Steven Edwards, The Bluebird Tea Co, Isaac At, Real Patisserie, Sussex Produce Co, and lots more.
978-1-910863-22-0

The South London Cook Book features Jose Pizarro, Adam Byatt, The Alma, Piccalilli Caff, Canopy Beer, Inkspot Brewery and lots more.
978-1-910863-27-5

The Bristol Cook Book features Dean Edwards, Lido, Clifton Sausage, The Ox, and wines from Corks of Cotham plus lots more.
978-1-910863-14-5

The Oxfordshire Cook Book features Mike North of The Nut Tree Inn, Sudbury House, Jacobs Inn, The Muddy Duck and lots more.
978-1-910863-08-4

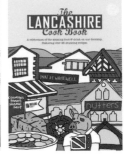

The Lancashire Cook Book features Andrew Nutter of Nutters Restaurant, Bertram's, The Blue Mallard and lots more.
978-1-910863-09-1

The Liverpool Cook Book features Burnt Truffle, The Art School, Fraîche, Villaggio Cucina and many more.
978-1-910863-15-2

The Sheffield Cook Book - Second Helpings features Jameson's Tea Rooms, Craft & Dough, The Wortley Arms, The Holt, Grind Café and lots more.
978-1-910863-16-9

The Leeds Cook Book features The Boxtree, Crafthouse, Stockdales of Yorkshire and lots more.
978-1-910863-18-3

The Cotswolds Cook Book features David Everitt-Matthias of Champignon Sauvage, Prithvi, Chef's Dozen and lots more.
978-0-9928981-9-9

The Shropshire Cook Book features Chris Burt of The Peach Tree, Old Downton Lodge, Shrewsbury Market, CSons and lots more.
978-1-910863-32-9

The Norfolk Cook Book features Richard Bainbridge, Morston Hall, The Duck Inn and lots more.
978-1-910863-01-5

The Lincolnshire Cook Book features Colin McGurran of Winteringham Fields, TV chef Rachel Green, San Pietro and lots more.
978-1-910863-05-3

The Newcastle Cook Book features David Coulson of Peace & Loaf, Bealim House, Grainger Market, Quilliam Brothers and lots more.
978-1-910863-04-6

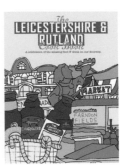

The Cheshire Cook Book features Simon Radley of The Chester Grosvenor, The Chef's Table, Great North Pie Co., Harthill Cookery School and lots more.
978-1-910863-07-7

The Leicestershire & Rutland Cook Book features Tim Hart of Hambleton Hall, John's House, Farndon Fields, Leicester Market, Walter Smith and lots more.
978-0-9928981-8-2

All books in this series are available from Waterstones, Amazon and independent bookshops.

FIND OUT MORE ABOUT US AT WWW.MEZEPUBLISHING.CO.UK